100 CHINESE SILENCES

First edition published in 2016 by Les Figues Press, Los Angeles.

Second edition published in 2024 by Les Figues, an imprint of punctum books, Earth, Milky Way.
https://punctumbooks.com

ISBN-13: 978-1-68571-222-8 (print)
ISBN-13: 978-1-68571-223-5 (ePDF)

DOI: 10.53288/0549.1.00

LCCN: 2024946544
Library of Congress Cataloging Data is available from the Library of Congress

Book design: Vincent W.J. van Gerven Oei

Les Figues is an imprint established under the punctum books Special Collections initiative.

Timothy Yu

100 Chinese Silences

LES FIGUES

Contents

To my mother
Linda Yu
and my grandmother
Sophia Pan

100 Chinese Silences

Chinese Silence No. 1

after Billy Collins, "Grave"

What do you think of this poem
I asked the tomb of my unknown grandfather
with its livid quiet marble.

A Chinese silence fell.
It dropped from a glowering tree
to perch on my shoulder.

We looked at each other.
It would have been hard for a stranger
to tell one of us from the other.

We both looked like monks or scholars
or like piles of drowned bones
laid softly on the loamy earth.

My grandfather said nothing.
His Chinese silence coiled its tail
into the shape of a long-lobed ear,

one of the one hundred American signs
for anxious virility.
Then the silence fell

into a cardboard box full of other silences.
Like blind puppies they squirmed
and snuffled for their mother.

OK, I made that last part up.
But you must admit it was a fabulous metaphor.
No? Oh, now I see

you are just as Chinese
as all the other silences—
the Silence of the Heavily Armed Gunboat,

or the Silence of the Drunken Mariner,
or my grandfather's silence, like the Liberty Bell,
only cracked right through.

Chinese Silence No. 2

after Billy Collins, "Old Man Eating Alone in a Chinese Restaurant"

I have resisted the temptation
to write a poem about an old man
eating alone at the unwiped counter
of an American restaurant.

The man's credit card has been declined.
He pats his pockets for change.
He finds nothing but an unread copy
of *A Coney Island of the Mind.*

I pass over in silence
the way the bacon smells like bacon
and heart disease here at Ed's
and how cold are the stares of the patrons.

The book, as it turns out, is actually
by Billy Collins. I open it
and find that it is a Chinese menu
of twice-cooked escalating horrors.

Which reminds me to mention the Chinese silence
that is slanting through the fogged-up windows
and falling through the skylight, quieting
the empty register and filthy tabletops,

as well as the curled black hair on the chest
of the cook in the bloody apron,
the one who turns his back on me
to hand a tuna melt to the shamed old man.

Chinese Silence No. 3

after Billy Collins, "Reading an Anthology of Chinese Poems of the Sung Dynasty, I Pause to Admire the Length and Clarity of Their Titles"

It seems this poet has nothing
up his empty sleeve
but a deck of Chinese flash cards,
each providing the first line
that makes an eye wet or dry,
shut or open, knee-deep in nature
or floating in a vat of wine.

Maybe he is choking on something he meant to swallow.
Maybe atomic fallout is blanketing New York.

"Viewing Penises Adjacent to Lotus Flowers
on a Sunday Afternoon" is one of his best-known works.
"Dipping My Finger in Tepid Tea"
is another one, but it's no
"Pagodas Keep Me Awake All Night."

And he takes the mother-loving apple pie with
"I Rode the Subway on a Sweaty Night
Carrying a Porcelain Vase.
It Was Very Sad and Seemed to Be Saying
Fill Me with Cruelty, or with One of Your Poems."

When he pushed against the bamboo turnstile
it didn't play "Wichita Vortex Sutra,"
"Me So Horny," or whatever.
It just laid there like a doormat.

So "I Walked Out on My Loving Wife
to the Sound of Temple Cash Registers"
is a wire brush kissing my lips.

And "Ten Days of Dysentery Have Kept Us Apart"
is a houseboy knocking his head on the floor
of a room where a poet with thinning hair
is sitting on a yoga mat with a bottle of Scotch
muttering something about China and nuclear wind,
about currency and hormone deficiencies.

He doesn't notice as I enter here,
pull up a barstool,
contort my spine like his, in silence.

Chinese Silence No. 4

after Billy Collins, "China"

I am a cicada floating in a coffee cup
on the desk of the Poet Laureate.

Grant proposals are being written.
Many bottles of Napa wine are emptied.

But even when his nodding head
strikes the desk like a bobbing Buddha's,

I lurk silently inside
my mug, chipped by the teeth of Ezra Pound.

Chinese Silence No. 5

Q: How would you define poetry?

A: Some people think poetry should be like garbage. This is standard workshop advice: poetry should be ripe and fetid as the air we breathe. I don't believe that. I say, keep the garbage where it belongs, on barges stranded off the coast of New Jersey. It's not part of the way the poem emerges, after much squeezing and straining, in one warm and continuous movement. It is not part of the poem's ****.

Q: What was that word you used?

A: ****. It's a term used in Feng Shui, Tai Chi, anime, and the Kama Sutra. It is a Chinese silence that runs through all things. Poems that don't have it are like machines made out of words, rusty and neurotic and full of language. Then you take them into workshop and try to fix them by revising. The Chinese never revise anything. As a great Chinese poet said, "You just go on your nerve." Well, I assume that's what he would have said if he could speak. He was sitting on a toilet at the time.

Q: Um, okay. How would you describe the ideal poet?

A: A heavily armed U.S. Marine.

Q: Excuse me?

A: Well, think about the haiku. There's a little haiku I like that says, "The cherry tree blooms. / I sigh into my latte: / A box of puppies." Basically what that says is, "I was here." Or "Kilroy was here." Which is what American soldiers liked to write on stuff in Japan and Korea. And the only reason we know about the haiku is because Commodore Perry sailed to Japan and said, "I am here. With a lot of big guns."

Q: Anything else?

A: I'm very good at playing with my own tail.

Q: Do you have any advice for a young Asian American poet?

A: [silence]

Chinese Silence No. 6

after Billy Collins, "Despair"

So much reserve and silence in our poetry.
Our words bloom like quiet peonies
looking at themselves in a covered mirror.

Our corpselike bodies cover the ground
and moan in the opium pipe,
yet our equanimity devours the air.

I wonder what my ancient Chinese predecessors
would make of all this,
these engineers and monkish masters?

Today, I hear your tinny voice blaring from the rooftops
in praise of my reticence, and my thoughts turn
to my honorable ancestors:

Fuk Yu, who gnashed Pacific rails
between his eloquent teeth,
and his great-grandson, glaring out from the Middle West,
Yu No-Hu.

Chinese Silence No. 7

after Billy Collins, "Liu Yung"

This poet of the American century is so amiable.
Commentators sigh on the radio
and a stealth bomber passes overhead
as he floats a model of the Titanic in his bathtub.

Now what if he approached life
with the same Chinese silence that I do?
No oompah-oompah from the podium,
no punchline in the parable.

The bird closes its tedious eye.
The cartoon clock stops the poet's mouth.

Chinese Silence No. 8

after Billy Collins, "Hangover"

If I were crowned Holy Roman Emperor this evening
every poet who speaks of Chinese silence
on National Public Radio
would be forced to mutter the name of Ezra Pound

Ezra Pound Ezra Pound

then be required to read the complete works
of Marianne Moore and write a dissertation
titled "'Superior People Never Make Long Visits':
Silence and Chinoiserie in the Poetry of

Marianne Moore Marianne Moore"

after which the poet would be quizzed
on Asian American poetry then executed by Zen
regardless of how many times he begged
for mercy calling upon the name of

Gary Snyder Gary Snyder

Chinese Silence No. 9

after Billy Collins, "Evening Alone"

Flickering tanning lamp
on white arms, bald white head,
muzak from the ceiling speakers,
and the prickle of air conditioning on his shoulders.

He turns his face to the bulb, closes his eyes
and sees flesh folded
over flesh,
dew beaded on a pair of silent thighs,
and in the distance, billowing smokestacks...

It must be the Bronx I am beholding
on this freezing late spring morning—
that gray plodding river of the East,
jet contrails carving the sky,
the cheers and bombers of the Bronx,
apartment towers—now the wail of a siren.

It is a vision that fills me with bile.
I want nothing
more than to be anywhere
other than his steamy Chinese poem
grinding my teeth, scratching my sides,

the words slithering silently down my throat and gut,
fogging my eyes,
while in the Bronx,
a light truck crosses the Throgs Neck Bridge,

and in a bar on the Jersey shore
a young woman in a Lycra dress
lifts a rum-filled cocktail
to her swollen lips.

Chinese Silence No. 10

after Billy Collins, "In the Room of a Thousand Miles"

I hate writing about where I am.
I happen to be sitting in a waiting room
full of anthologies of translated Chinese poetry
and no window.
So I will write about the pink trees of China
and their small, nervous puppies.
I will pour myself
a cup of Tab
or Sierra Mist
and write that it is rice wine.

My reader hands these poems back to me
with a groan.
She wants to drill a hole
in my skull.
She suggests I write some
conceptualist orientalism
or do a Google search
for "ancient Chinese girls."
I ignore her.
Instead I return
to my vinyl chair.
I think about the furniture of the Chinese,
their globular buttocks, their polluted cities.
I visualize a dragon swallowing San Francisco,
gnawing the Golden Gate, choking on Coit Tower.
And then—don't tell anyone—
I smile into my diet cola
and in the manner of the ancient Chinese
pick up my dried-out pen
and tattoo on the skin of my palm
a character that means
"A journey of a thousand miles
is really, really long."

Chinese Silence No. 11

after Billy Collins, "Drawing"

Graffiti on the girders
of a rusted bridge
over a sewage channel,

tenements in the distance
and in the foreground
a burned-out car.

I turn the picture upside down.
Now it looks Chinese,
burrowing silently earthward.

Chinese Silence No. 12

after Billy Collins, "Shoveling Snow with Buddha"

On the airwaves of your local listener-supported public radio station
he would never be caught dead doing such a thing,
tossing his own words into a pile
over his slumping shoulder,
forming a knot
of concentrated failure.

Glibness is more his speed, if that is the word
for what he does, or does not do.

The setting is all wrong for him.
In all his appearances, is the compensation not more than generous?
Is this not evident in his smug expression,
the smirk that forms the axis of the poetic universe?

But here we are, working our way through an anthology of Asian
 American poetry,
one cliché at a time.
We read poems about silent grandmothers in the kitchen.
We smell the aromas of their wok-fired cooking.
And with the turn of every page
we are lost to each other
in these sudden clouds of our own meaning,
these machine-gun bursts of solipsism.

This is so much better than the usual Orientalism,
I say out loud, but he keeps on reading.
This is true Asian American writing,
where everyone is always "caught between cultures,"
I say, but he ignores me.

He is gulping down these Asian American poems
as if being Asian were the purpose of his existence,
as if the sign of a perfect life were an ink-brush painting
hanging from the rear-view mirror,
blocking your view of the American road,
tuning the radio to The Top 100 Chinese Silences.

All morning we read side by side,
me with my commentary
and he shushing me into silence,
until the book is finished
and its pages lie discarded all around us;
then, I hear him speak.

Is not each of these poems, he asks,
itself a form of Chinese silence?

Actually, no, I reply, each is a testament
to the noise of being Asian in America.
To silence them would be to erase them
into blank pages for your own projections.

Ah so, he says, shaking his bottle of White-Out
and poising the wet brush over the poem,
then spreading the pungent liquid over the page
until the words are silenced.

Chinese Silence No. 13

after Billy Collins, "A Portrait of the Reader with a Bowl of Cereal"

Every morning I sit across from him
at the curio table,
halogen lamps lighting all the bric-à-brac:
curve of a knockoff Ming vase,
a bowl of lychees—
me in a scholar's gown or kimono,
he inscrutable.

Most days, we are suspended
in a deep Chinese silence.
He stares straight through me,
imagining his sailboat on the Yellow River
with its steel-tipped masts
drawing erotic graffiti in the inkbrush sky.

I offer him egg rolls,
chicken fried rice,
and cups of oolong tea,
but he hides behind his copy
of Ezra Pound's *Cathay*.

But some days I may notice
a little door swinging open
in his balding skull,
revealing his dreams
of brocade-clad maidens
sliding down the china slope of his mind—

then I will lean forward,
delicate fingers trembling,
to trace a shriek of *Aiiieeeee!*
on his folded gray matter
as my words drip from his docile lips.

Chinese Silence No. 14

after Billy Collins, "Silence"

You have the right to remain silent.
That is your job.
A ball gag plugs your mouth,
and the immigrant girl with her loud
sewing machine has been deported.

So tell us about the mind of China.
We want to hear the silent blooming of its cherry blossoms,
the quiet unfastening of its gowns,
its songs of soy sauce
and tiny bound feet.

Its trains have been blown up by dynamite,
its factories bombed into silence.
Its mewling puppies have been smothered
and its gods are suffocating inside specimen jars.
Shanghai has been evacuated

and each inhabitant issued an edition of Gary Snyder.
So tell us about your ancestors,
your grandfather in his bamboo cage,
your grandmother drowned in the well.
Let's hear about the unmoving clouds, the stunted trees.

Read the poem we have placed in front of you.
The Pacific has been drained,
and even Ezra Pound
has burst from his grave,
his moldering hand poised to translate what you do not say.

Chinese Silence No. 15

after Billy Collins, "Bonsai"

All it takes is him to throw a room
totally out of whack.

As he looks out the window
it turns into a bamboo screen

that shows him stark naked
floating in a distant rice paddy.

Up close, he almost looks Chinese,
everything cut down to size.

But when he steps back to the doorway,
he is American again, dilated and bloated.

The top button of his discarded dress shirt
is the turning wheel

of a steamboat thrashing the Yangtze River,
and his coffee cup a well

to catch the desires
that moisten his tightened mouth.

He even makes the weather Chinese,
his gray hair spinning in a typhoon gust

that blows silence
through the puppies of the Bronx.

The Whitestone Bridge bends eastward
like a bonsai tree

and he climbs its sagging supports,
holding on for dear life

as it folds inward like his belly's flesh
and his tiny whale dives beneath the waves.

If only he could plunge his body
into a warm and silent Chinese ditch,

instead of being trapped in the Lexington Avenue subway tunnel
for the next one thousand years.

Chinese Silence No. 16

after Billy Collins, "Japan"

Today I pass the time reciting
your favorite Chinese poem,
saying the silent words over and over.

It feels like jumping
up and down on little bound feet
again and again.

I walk through your house repeating it
and leave its silence falling
on your furniture like ash.

I stand next to your silent alarm system and say it.
I say it in front of your flat-screen TV showing *Crouching Tiger, Hidden Dragon.*
I tap out its rhythm with a pair of chopsticks.

I listen to myself saying it,
but of course I don't hear anything
inside my Chinese silence.

And when the squealing puppies look up at me,
I kneel down on the floor
and think about dinner.

The poem is the one about the little
China girl
lying silent on the beach

feeling the excruciating
pressure of your body
all over her porcelain skin.

You like to imagine
her body is a temple bell
chiming under the weight of your eyes.

But when you look in the mirror
your head has taken on the shape of a bell,
your shoulders bending downward like a fortune cookie.

And when your tongue tries
to ring out a cry
for help against your cast-iron palate,

she rises from the bed, saying
shhhhh, baby,
just shut your mouth.

Chinese Silence No. 17

after Billy Collins, "Reincarnation and You"

Reincarnation is such an outlandish idea.
It must have been invented by some elephant-headed god
beside a noisy Indian river.

But if I had to pick something
to come back as
I guess I would be Chinese.

I admire the quiet modesty of their lives.
I revere their silent consumption
of cicadas, pigeons, and household pets.

Or maybe I would come back as a waterfall
of wispy hair spilling from the chin
of a Chinese sage, the fine strands

quivering with the silent motions of his mouth.
A jade ox, I will say one day,
and the next a puddle of urine

in a rural village with unspeakable sanitation.
Or I will pick a peach of immortality
and hang there forever in the Chinese sun

laughing at Americans with their silly deaths
from heart disease and boredom
as they sit there before their television sets

with puppies in their laps.
But never mind all that,
never mind my kung-fu panda fantasies

of being a Chinese soul.
Forget that silent afterlife
with its muted desires.

Come and look into my rheumy blue eyes.
Tell me you are opening your kimono
and removing the chopsticks holding up your smooth black hair

and I will whisper in your ear
what I really want to be, come to think of it,
which is a grinning white tiger

entering the cage of your silent zoo,
tenderly mauling your almond face
as you weep with quiet pleasure,

then devouring your bamboo-thin limbs
and lying down on the couch to digest,
waiting for you to be reborn in my poem.

Chinese Silence No. 18

after Billy Collins, "Bodhidharma"

This morning the surface of the Cross Bronx Expressway
is uncommonly crowded—absolutely jammed—
which must be the reason I am thinking
of Gary, the man who brought Buddhism
to America by crossing the water standing on Ezra Pound's head.

What an absorbing story, especially
when you compare it to Manzanar with its barbed-wire fence
or the walls of Angel Island's barracks
that can't decide whether to hold you in or send you back.

In every depiction, there is no mistaking
Gary, pounding away with his axe,
cruising the American lake in his powerboat,

his beard sharpened like a stone
precariously balanced beneath two Chinese checkers
as he paints mountains and rivers without end
in the pages of a New Directions paperback.

I recognized him one night in City Lights Bookstore
after the disappointment
of not meeting any Chinese girls reading silent haiku in the aisles.

His picture was hanging behind the cash register,
and when I quizzed the young cashier,
he looked back at the photo and said
he didn't know who it was but it looked kind of like Mr. Miyagi.

Thinking of Mr. Miyagi and of Chinese girls
makes me want to do many things,
but mostly to strip off my clothes
and body surf or ride a jet ski
to the silent shores of China.

My wallet would have been left behind,
but I can think of a way to make money.
I would announce to the silent Chinese billions
that it is foolish to invest too heavily
in infrastructure and export factories,

not when they have the benefit of me
with my great pillowed thighs to remind them
of the quiet mind
that Gary borrowed from them
and that I'll happily give them back
for only a small markup, no questions asked.

Chinese Silence No. 19

after Billy Collins, "Kathmandu"

It was sleeting in Madison, Wisconsin,
and hail was falling in Duluth,
but still, the access roads to the malls
were thick with station wagons,
all waiting for the books of the Laureate,
whose title pages had been smeared with ink
by the thumb of the poet,
to smear their words across the mild brains
of these Sunday crossword solvers.

Don't worry, there are plenty of copies,
the kid at the cell-phone kiosk said
as he laid out headsets and Blackberries
assembled by silent Chinese fingers.
The woman at the Dead Sea minerals booth agreed,
pouring out exfoliant scrubs and mud soaps
onto the desiccated floor.

But still they waited, hunkered down
in their Subarus with windshield wipers flapping,
hoping to make a connection
the way one might hope to be connected
by a long chain of allusions
to Ezra Pound and Li Po
only without the need to read
anything dull or unpleasant.

Meanwhile the Laureate is riding
in the backseat of a New York taxi
blackening his lashes with ink
and pulling his eyes up at the corners,
demonstrating to his driver his belief
that someday we will all turn Chinese
and that we go to China when we die—
a silent realm of modest ink-drawn birds,
a middlebrow kingdom of solipsism.

The driver, the Laureate thinks, must understand this
because he is already Chinese,
and although he is not wearing a funny hat
he receives the words with an authentic silence.

The Laureate's words smear the glass
as the driver looks out the fogged-up windows
at the obese children,
the teenagers shuffling along in their flip-flops,
ears plugged by headphones,
and in front of the bookstore, public-radio listeners
huddling together in the rain,
awaiting their Chinese afterlives.

Chinese Silence No. 20

> *This year July has 5 Fridays 5 Saturdays and 5 Sundays. This happens once every 823 years. This is called money bags. So copy this to your status and money will arrive within 4 days. Based on Chinese philosophy of Feng Shui. Those who read and do not copy will be without money.*
>
> —Facebook meme

I did not copy this
so I am without money.

But that is OK.
The ancient Chinese
philosophy of Feng Shui

tells me that every 551,557,906,200 oscillations
of a cesium-133 atom
an unenlightened soul is born.

This is called capitalism.
So every 886.245 hours
I deposit my poems

in the maw of a silent mailbox
and hope someone will buy them within 4 days.
This is called optimism.

But anyway, the ancient Chinese philosophy
of Tai Chi tells me
that "silence is its own reward,"

so I grow wealthier from rejection.
If you read this
and do not copy

you will be cursed by the words
of the ancient Chinese sage Dong Le:
"He who cannot afford to speak

must remain silent."

Chinese Silence No. 21

after Billy Collins, "Air Piano"

Now that all the America has seeped
out of the room
and a Chinese silence has fallen,

my father's voice
becomes an angry zither
twanging about filial piety,

always the same tune
from dawn to dusk,
enough to build a culture on.

My ex-wife's figure
with its ponderous hands and feet
turns into a tiny lotus blossom.

If you didn't like those metaphors, don't worry,
I have lots more of them,
one for every inhabitant of China.

Like when I compare
my little brother
to a barbarian from the West

silently skewered by a bamboo spear.
But I—
I am the same I

I always was, just in Chinese drag,
my swelling curves hugged
by a tight red gown,

feet tightly bound
as I totter around the house
nibbling on lychees and fortune cookies.

I have learned to say *ni hao*
and *gwai lo*,
but what I really love is lying here

in silence,
delicate hands dancing in the air
playing "Chopsticks"

and watching myself in the mirror
as if I were my own fantasy,
another metaphor forming on my smiling lips.

Chinese Silence No. 22

after Billy Collins, "Monday"

The Italians are making their pasta,
the French are making things French,
and the Chinese cultivate their silence.

They cultivate silence
in every Chinatown on the persimmon of earth—
mute below the towers of Toronto,
silently sweeping the streets of Singapore
clear of noisy self-expression.

The Americans are in their sport utility vehicles,
the Canadians are behaving reasonably,
but the Chinese remain silent
maybe with a cup of tea or an opium pipe
and maybe a finger puzzle or water torture is involved.

Or maybe the Chinese are playing the Chinese
game of ping-pong,
the pock-pock of the ball against their tight-lipped mouths
as their chefs dice scallions and bean curd.
The Chinese are silent
because it is their job for which
I pay them what they got for building the railroads.

Which silence it is hardly seems to matter
though many have a favorite
out of the 100 different kinds—
the Silence of the Well-Adjusted Minority,
the Girlish Silence of Reluctant Acquiescence,
the Silence that by No Means Should Be Mistaken for Bitterness.

By now, it should go without saying
that what Crocodile Dundee is to the Australian
and Mel Gibson is to the Scot,
so is silence to the Chinese.

Just think—
before I invented the 100 Chinese silences,
the Chinese would have had to stay indoors
and gabble about civil war and revolution
or go outside and build a really loud wall.

And when I say a wall,
I do not mean a wall of thousands of miles
that is visible from the moon.

I mean a noisy wall of language
that dwarfs my medieval battlements
and paves the Pacific to lap
California's shores with its brick-hard words.

Chinese Silence No. 23

after Billy Collins, "The Day Lassie Died"
(which is of course after Frank O'Hara, "The Day Lady Died")

It is 12:20 am in Beijing a Thursday
two months after the bicentennial of our nation, yes
it is 1976 and I write some poems
that sound like what a third-rate Wallace Stevens
would think up after getting off the 7:15 in Hartford
and then not even bother writing down before going in to dinner

I stop into YU HU'S NEW YORK CHINESE CAFE
and have egg foo yung and moo shu pork and open
my ugly fortune cookie to see what the poets
in China are saying these days
                                        I go on to the laundry
and Mr. Lee (first name or last name, who knows)
hands over my shirts with a side of silence
and in the CHINATOWN ORIENTAL BOOKSTORE
I get a little Li Po with erotic drawings for myself
along with *Zen and the Art of Motorcycle Maintenance*
and I don't see *On Contradiction* or "Serve
the People," I keep my eyes on Li Po
and fall into an exotic silence

and to assure my future as POET LAUREATE
I stroll into a Buddhist temple and ask them
if they will help me shovel snow and they
tell me to go back where I came from so
I walk out with a carton of incense and some lady
slaps me with a little red book with his name on it

and I am crying a lot now and thinking of
urinating in the alley behind the 4 SPOT
while he rose from his bed to shake the hand
of Dick Nixon and everyone and I fell silent

Chinese Silence No. 24

after David Sedaris, "Chicken Toenails, Anyone?"

We are all just animals
a pinch of human feces
scrambled eggs duck tongues
tentacle-like roots

What do you say
we go oriental?
And the egg rolls...
can you imagine?

They allowed you to brown bag
wads of phlegm
in the men's room of a Beijing subway station
I looked at her thinking, You whore

I have to go to China
I've never looked forward to it
like twice-baked potatoes
or veal parmesan

It's more real
I could dislike it
more authentically
than the sound of one person

then another
dredging up seeming
from the depths of my soul
using the other as a blowhole

In China something kept holding me back
the leg, the breast, etc.
hacked as if by a blind person
made entirely of organs

Yes, I must
shit in the produce aisle of a Chengdu Walmart
Yes, I must
disintegrate in the western-style toilet

Chinese Silence No. 25

after David Sedaris, "Chicken Toenails, Anyone?"

I hurt that Tokyo, where the food was bathrooms,
Everything so younger I had to pee all the time
That odd incessant guttural hiss from the depths
Of his or her soul. Where are you going
To put that? I saw wads of Chinese
Plugging one nostril back into his pocket
(A sanitary consideration) oh please turds must you?
Yes I must, strange little pants with a slit in the rear.
So desensitized was I.

Another thing one notices in China is the thinking.
Stuff comes out of every hole we have
Shove it to the back of our minds and nailed.
There wasn't a lot of familiar in China
(one Chinese woman and three westerners
a simmering cauldron of broth)
I've taken the liberty of ordering
Do you trust me to keep ordering?

When I was eventually forced quackless
I took a drive to the mountain where tea
Originally came from. We ran thick with
Waste and rubbish. The people who live there
Will serve you if they're in the mood.

I spoke Mandarin square-faced and pretty.
There was a rooster, then there wasn't.
Nothing else was nearly as recognizable
As the heart that so disgusted me
The thing that sits on top of the head
Doing nothing

Raised on corn or horrible chemicals
Pigs and dead people are distinctions
Made in China. Oh those poor things
How could you?
                                        I went, "Huh?"
I didn't say anything.

Chinese Silence No. 26

for Wendi Deng

tiger tiger tiger wife
wonder woman volleyball spike
if you have an Asian wife
maybe she's not just a gold-digger?

tiger wife or trophy wife?
slam-down sister or socialite?
bright pink jacket and pencil skirt
not like gold-digger who wants old man hurt

Wendi Deng is a Power Ranger
with Crazy Asian Magic Powers
was in Red Army? trained to kill?
agile PYT hit like a girl

Crouching tiger? flying Murdoch?
tiger wife clawed her way up
Chinese bloggers catch Deng fever
Wendy Daaaang her homegirls call her

thank you for everything #mrmiyagi
business school graduate? yoga devotee?
from communist obscurity
"herro you rike pilate DVD?"

tiger tiger tiger wife
wonder woman volleyball spike
if you have an Asian wife
what if she's not just a gold-digger?

Chinese Silence No. 27

after David Ferry, "Little Vietnam Futurist Poem"

I come into your ear as loud as
Some teenage pop song gone all wrong,
Trumpeting the malfunctions of my eye.

Birdbrained. Sickly laughing. Removing your pajamas.
Reveling in my dreadfulness.
Pulling out something, extracting something or other

From your little mouth in a guilty fever.
Of course you don't want to hear the words I am saying
Because I am evil. But I've got you in my sight.

No really, just stay there in your Chinese pajamas.
I know I am just some asshole or other
Made up by the nice man who is writing me.

This is a conversation we're having between ourselves.
So just keep quiet while we tell you how it was.

Chinese Silence No. 28

after Eliot Weinberger, "The Cloud Bookcase"

The Chinaman Bookcase

An Australian in China: Being the Narrative of a Quiet Journey across China to Burma
by George Ernest Morrison M.D.Edin., F.R.G.S. (1895)
Remarks on the character of the Cantonese, Chinese emigrants, cretins, and wife-beating in China.

Battle Hymn of the Tiger Mother
by Amy Chua (2011)
Western parents are concerned about their children's psyches. Chinese parents aren't.

The British Quarterly Review
Vol. 53–54 (1871)
The Chinese people sadly lack truth, uprightness, and honour, the fear of God.

Bulletin of the Atomic Scientists, vol. 39
Anonymous (1983)
Everyone who studies China has a hidden China in his heart.

The Chinese as they are: their moral, social, and literary character. A new analysis of the language; with succinct views of their principal arts and sciences
by George Tradescant Lay (1841)
The face of a Chinese female is distinguished by its breadth, and the smallness of the mouth, nose, and eyes. There is an apparent vacancy, or at least a great lack of expression. But the smile of a Chinese woman is inexpressibly charming; we seldom see anything like it, save when the feelings of delight and complacency beam from the eyes of a wife or mistress upon the object of her choice.

Chinese Dental Methods
by D.V.F. (1902)
If you want the filling to stay in for any length of time, don't go to an "almond-eyed" dentist. How do you think you would like to have your teeth "repaired" by Dr. John Chinaman?

The Chinese in America
by Otis Gibson (1877)
The Chinese maiden, before marriage, is kept in seclusion and ignorance. The principal lesson she has to learn is obedience.

The Chinese Mind: Essentials of Chinese Philosophy and Culture
edited by Charles A. Moore (1967)
To understand the contemporary world of Asia—and to be able to live at peace, or at war, if need be, with any other people—we must know them.

Chinese Sexual Astrology: Eastern Secrets to Mind-Blowing Sex
by Shelly Wu (2006)
Chinese sexual astrology contains tried-and-true advice that combines spiritual compatibility with physical pleasures, from the erotic imagery of tomb decorations to the 10th century crystal penis.

Debates, House of Commons, Dominion of Canada, 5th Parliament, 3rd Session
by Douglas Benjamin Woodworth (1885)
A dirty, greasy man, a man with a long pigtail hanging down his back, unfit for human society, with a forbidding countenance, with a flat head, with pinched toes.

Dissertations Moral and Critical
by James Beattie (1783)
The Chinese mode of building has no pretensions to sublimity; its decorations being still more trivial than the Gothic; and because it derives no dignity from associated ideas, and has not vastness of magnitude to raise admiration.

Doing Business in China: The Sun Tzu Way
by Laurence J. Brahm (2004)
Businessmen traveling regularly to China often find "second wives" or concubines. The girls in Sichuan are very pretty, but they are not stupid.

The dragon, image, and demon: or, The three religions of China
by Hampden C. Dubose (1886)
China the Land of Demons.—Evil spirits flit hither and thither. Each Chinaman has three souls. We are compassed about with so great a cloud of demons.

Dreaming in Chinese: Mandarin lessons in life, love, and language
by Deborah Fallows (2010)
Chinese can be very superstitious about names. One of my friends had a boyfriend whose parents, according to a peasant custom, named him "pile of shit."

Europe in China: the history of Hongkong from the beginning to the year 1882
by Ernest John Eitel (1895)
The Continent of Asia juts out into the Pacific, as if beckoning to the rest of the world to come on.

Fixing Sex: Intersex, Medical Authority, and Lived Experience
by Katrina Alicia Karkazis (2008)
Using the definition of micro-penis as roughly 2.5 centimeters in length, the authors obtained values of 2.6, 2.5, and 2.3 centimeters for newborns of Caucasian, East Indian, and Chinese background, respectively. The authors concluded that mean penile length and diameter are slightly but significantly smaller in newborns of Chinese origin.

Forest and Stream: A Weekly Journal of the Rod and Gun
(1895)
He describes such non-resident discriminations as "un-American, Chinese, selfish, brutally discourteous."

The Gary Snyder reader: prose, poetry, and translations, 1952-1998
by Gary Snyder (2000)
I still have doubts about China. I feel ambivalent about China.

How to Do Business in China: 24 Lessons to Make Working in China More Profitable
by Nick Dallas (2008)
Knowledge is power and ignorance isn't bliss. Don't just swallow the hype about China. Convince yourself of the China story. Visit blog sites. Arm yourself with an arsenal of knowledge. It's amazing what random word searches on the Web can reveal.

The Importance of Being Charlie Chan
by Sandra M. Hawley (1991)
When American and Chinese characteristics are compared, it is usually the American rush against the Chinese calm, American ambition against Chinese acceptance and serenity.

Importance of the Teleological Argument
by Rev. C.F. Kupfer, D.D. (1872)
To the Chinese mind God is hidden. The Bible is not sacred to him; he is prejudiced against it.

Mao Zedong Was a Yale Grad and Other Conspiracies of the Obscure
by Sean Vermillion (2008)
The reason why Chinese take-out and delivery restaurants are all virtually the same is because they belong to a national company that is partly owned by the Reverend Sun Myung Moon and functions as a front for the CIA and Taiwanese intelligence.

Mission stories of many lands: A book for young people. With three hundred and forty illustrations
American Board of Commissioners for Foreign Missions (1885)
Children can be good and honor their parents without doing the strange and often wicked things which the Chinese often recommend.

Modern Chinese Secret
by Mary Carroll (1993)
Once you've mastered a few ancient Chinese secrets, there'll be no more Jimmy Wu's for you.

Mysteries of the life force: my apprenticeship with a Chi kung master
by Peter Meech (2007)
"Oh, you not lose Western brain. Just gain Chinese brain."
"But what if I don't want a Chinese brain?"
"Oh, this too late. Already have one. Didn't notice?"

The Mysterious Chinese Book of Everything
by Tim Casart (2005)
"There is even an entry for seeing two gay dogs doing nasty with each other."

Poetics of Emptiness: Transformations of Asian Thought in American Poetry
by Jonathan Stalling (2010)
When first encountering the poetics of emptiness, one will likely draw strong connections to Gary Snyder.

Rhus vernicifera.—A note from Hong Kong
by W.J. Tutcher (1901)
An empty cigar box makes a first-rate pillow for a Chinaman.

A String of Chinese Peach-Stones
by William Arthur Cornaby (1895)
Most "mandarin Chinese" sounds are at one time or another uttered by infants the wide world over. We all begin life by talking Chinese.

Ten thousand things on China and the Chinese: being a picture of the genius, government, history, literature, agriculture, arts, trade, manners, customs, and social life of the people of the Celestial Empire as illustrated by the Chinese collection, 539 Broadway
by J.S. Redfield (1850)
Barnum's Chinese Museum.—Barnum's enterprise stops short of nothing that is strange or wonderful. How he could tempt a Chinese lady of unquestionable character and position to travel among the "outside barbarians," and how he could smuggle her out of that mysterious country, no one can imagine; yet he has done both. Miss Pwan-Yekoo, the Chinese belle, with her Chinese suite of attendants, is drawing all Broadway to the Chinese collection. She is so pretty, so arch, so lively, and so graceful, while her minute feet are wondrous!

Things Chinese: being notes on various subjects connected with China
by James Dyer Ball (1900) and others
France appears desirous of penetrating China. France is penetrating China from the south. It is absolutely necessary for us to have a railway penetrating China. Our great missionary interests penetrating China with the slogan "Let there be Light." Diseases jumping borders and penetrating China. Preventing Bolshevism from penetrating China. Holding back the Protestants of Europe from penetrating China. Prostitutes are the playthings of foreign exploiters who are literally penetrating China.

Tramping on Life: An Autobiographical Narrative
by Harry Kemp (1922)
I used to have to take the boathook and push off the Chinese corpses that caught on the prow of the boat as they floated down, thick...they seemed to catch hold of the prow as if still alive.

The United States Marines in North China, 1894-1942
by Chester M. Biggs (2003)
Conditions worsened. Sanitation was abominable. Chinese corpses and dead horses and dogs were scattered beyond the defense lines.

The Way of the Fertile Soul: Ten Ancient Chinese Secrets to Tap Into a Woman's Creative Potential
by Randine Lewis (2007)
I was hooked on the benefits of Oriental medicine. This program is based on the ten secrets of healthful living that I discovered in the ancient tomes.

The writing of weddings in middle-period China: text and ritual practice in the eighth through fourteenth centuries
by Christian De Pee (2007)
Medical concern with loss of semen. Emission control and emission quotas. Male weakness resulting from loss of semen. Sexual possession and rape of adult women. Impregnated virgins. Even statues and paintings of women may be impregnated.

www.hotcute.cn
Anonymous (21st century)
I am a Chinese girl. I am a beautiful Chinese girl, a hot but very cute girl. I love the world, I love peaceful!

Chinese Silence No. 29

I feel sorry for baby turtles.
They're like Chinese babies.
Toddler troops tottering through American streets
With AK-47s.

I knew by supernatural revelation from heaven
That I had a baby in China waiting.

Given the nature of the evidence
We must proceed under the assumption
That the Chinese are no more inclined to eat babies
Than folks who live anywhere else in the world.

Hipster Asian babies are the future.
For some reason they just turn out cuter
Than your average baby.
They're not just babies, they're Chinese babies.

I've made a decision to adopt 2 Chinese babies.
That way, not only do I get a $10,000 tax credit,
But I can name them Yu Ho and Ug Li
And it would not be inappropriate.

Does U.S. law treat Chinese babies
Like stolen cars?

Half Chinese babies are famous in China.
Half Chinese cute baby famous baby
Eurasian Hapa baby playing
& singing to the power points electricity outlet.

Half Chinese half Asian baby
Eats a Tootsie Roll with the wrapper on
And attempts to pull a fire alarm
At the Olive Garden.

I feel Asians are genetically superior.
And since my son is half white I'm trying
To force it out of him by making him play
Arcade dance games as all true Asians should.

WHy does it has American last name? not Asian?
Because her mom is Asian.

Chinese babies invading the America?
Now some Chinese babies are growing breasts.
I love fat Chinese babies!
Nothing kinky, just funny and cute.

Chinese Silence No. 30

after Eleanor Goodman, "Boston's Chinatown"

It's easy to slam the Chinatowns of America.
They're just a lot of red lanterns.
Yeah, there are Chinese people around,
But it's all for tourists.

Their dirty alleyways remind me
Of that strange beast called American culture.
The peculiar smell of fish (how Chinese!)—
I've eaten hundreds of meals there.

So I move on to mock the shantytowns of Asia.
They're just a lot of plywood and scrap metal.
Sure, I know there are poor people around.
I've seen *Slumdog Millionaire*.

I know the area pretty well.
I've hung out in "bad" neighborhoods before
Where the old men run their sketchy basement stores.
But they have mostly disappeared.

And it's all too tempting to denigrate
The postindustrial towns of the dull Midwest.
Of course I know there are unemployed people there.
I heard it on NPR.

Once I had to spend three hours
In the Detroit airport, with its vendors peddling
Chewing gum and soda.
But people don't really live there.

Just don't ask me to smash the glittering cities
Of cultural imperialism.
They teach English language skills
And how to adjust to life in the States.

Nobody really lives here.
As someone involved in translation
I've eaten hundreds of meals here.
Nobody speaks Chinese.

Chinese Silence No. 31

after Tom Clark, "Sounding Chinese at Inspiration Point""

Me like write poem sound Chinese
Like Charlie Chan read Fu Manchu
So get drunk on Grant Avenue

Chinese good at being silent
Not like ugga bugga barbarian
So put on coolie hat and bucktooth smile

Me say two Wongs can make it white
As stars in big Oriental sky
Because me afraid to think own thoughts

USA poet not so good these days
So learn lesson from ancient Chinese sage
And write poem like slant-eyed Kerouac

Chinese Silence No. 32

after Alan Shapiro, "Flowerpot"

I lie back in the sagging mattress that
Holds the bell of my body like a bell
Unrung for fifty years, and wonder

If it's still okay to call someone a "Chinaman."
I guess these days they don't all wear coolie hats
And hide their blushing faces behind bamboo fans,

But when I turn on my television they all still look
The same, the same as when Fu Manchu
Ran his long fingernails across a white man's chest.

Someone is saying something about
The balance of payments and our national debt.
I remember when it was just the Russian bomb

That scared us, and not the silent Chinaman
(I can say that, right?), dark empty eyes
Slanting down into the void.

I fear that he will swallow me whole,
My snuffling nose, my trembling arms,
My bones in the rickshaw of his gut.

And everything in the world I know
Falls like a hail of missiles into
The Chinaman stomach that will never fill.

Chinese Silence No. 33

after Biddy Jenkinson, "The Chinese Mother's Lullaby"

Pull up a chair, little China doll,
so I can kiss your tiny bound feet
while I explain to you why
I always use you as an example
whenever I want to make
a really dramatic point
about the oppression of women.
Sit still, don't be naughty.

Now you see, my little lotus blossom,
our modern Western society
has embraced words like "equality"
that you probably don't understand.
But sometimes we need to be
reminded how good we have it
through a comparison
to your dear, primitive culture.

You say the Chinese don't
bind feet anymore? No matter.
I will snap and crack
your tiny toes myself
until they break
like brittle bamboo,
then wrap them in smug
swaddlings of silk.

Now your poor dear feet
look nothing like my huge ones.
Of course you don't cry out.
I'm glad Chinese girls
have been raised to be quiet.
Just hold still. I'm doing this
for the benefit of women everywhere.
I'm doing this for your sake.

Chinese Silence No. 34

Asian–white pairings, especially Asian women and white men, are so common many "don't even look at that at all," says Kevin Noble Maillard, associate professor of law at Syracuse University in New York.

—*USA Today*, November 7, 2011

But what I see most often is,
white men with asian women.
The key is to focus
on a market-driven analysis.

I'm certainly not the first person to make this observation.
Dating is like going to the mall food court.
I've been to Burger King, Panda House,
New Delhi, and Taco Bell.

The Asians are what were once called "ladies."
You will frequently hear phrases like,
"He's a fucking piece of shit."
They do like being women.

seems like everywhere I go,
I see a white guy with asian girlfriend/wife?
gender asymmetries can be explained by
the universal preference for "taller husband"!

Its like a af/wm convention out there.
she kinda turned her face away
as if she was embarrassed or had guilt or something
all but maybe 2 of them have White husbands

Basically, Asian women look at white men
the same way white men look at Asian women,
like a white parody of yellow men,
only in whiteface.

White girl looking for SAM.
It's simple and it's free.
We won't be at all surprised if you entertained
thoughts of polygamy before making your final selection!

How nice it would be if my boyfriend
and I could switch ethnicities.
Asian women and fat white men.
Our kids will look Hispanic.

Chinese Silence No. 35

after Dan Gerber, "Often I Imagine the Earth"

Often I run out of ideas
for poems and the metaphors they're made of—
clichés, dull
clichés everywhere—
but then I remember I am an American
and so can end my poem with something Chinese
and call it original, like that
ancient American railroad
built miraculously by silent hands,
helping me drive my golden spike home.

Chinese Silence No. 36

> *To make a Chinese poem in English we must allow the silence to creep in around the edges, to define the words the way the sky's negative space in a painting defines the mountains.*
>
> —Tony Barnstone, "The Poem Behind the Poem"

To make a Japanese poem in English
we must allow the silence to creep up upon us
the way the ninja stalks and strangles
his unsuspecting victim.

To make an Indian poem in English
we must allow the waters of language to rise
and drown us like the Ganges until
we are reborn in a more accessible form.

To make a French poem in English
we must impale ourselves upon the Tour Eiffel
until our bloodcurdling screams evoke that sublime
je ne sais quoi.

To make a Spanish poem in English
we must let ourselves be gored by the charging bull
of poesy as we run like idiots through the streets
waving to our friends' cameras.

To make an American poem in English
we must level the mountains of language with dynamite
and in the rubble build an ethnic theme park
of charming accents and seething quiet.

To make an American poem Chinese
we must silence its creepy edges
and raise an iron-built mountain that mirrors
our own negation to us as if it were gold.

Chinese Silence No. 37

after Tony Barnstone, "Get Zen"

Get laid, you think. Or try. Indulge your lusts.
Think of a joke: What do you say to Freud
when he comes to your wiener stand, bill poised
for payment? "Sometimes a hot dog is just
a hot dog." Easier to close your eyes
and think of Buddha, roly-poly gut
and empty loins—he's kind of like you but
on purpose, not a loser full of sighs.
Gratification is a young man's game.
Now that you're old, it's time to turn Chinese
and cultivate a neutered silence. Please
to make an Eastern virtue of your sad-
sack self! You don't really think desire's bad;
self-pity's just better in Buddha's name.

Chinese Silence No. 38

after Gary Snyder, "Axe Handles"

One afternoon the second week in December
My son is throwing a hissyfit
Turning and turning like a routed stump.
He's got it in his hatchet-head
That he wants to go shopping, he can't get a handle
On himself, on his own backside.
I grab him by his ass handle
And swing him back like a hatchet,
Thinking to cut him down to size
And get it through his head
That he's this close to a trip to the woodshed.
So I begin to tell him about the Chinese
And their patient silence, the silence
Learned from Ezra Pound
At Rapallo:
"C'est moi
            dans la poubelle"
And I say this to the kid
"Look: I'm gonna slap your handle
With my handle
And the ass it rode in on—"
And he sees. And I hear it again:
It's in *A Draft of XVI Cantos*, 1924
A.D., Canto XIV—in the
First stanza: "Faces smeared on their rumps,
            wide eye on flat buttock,
Bush hanging for beard,
            Addressing crowds through their arse-holes."
I translated that into Chinese
And taught it to Americans
And I see: Pound was an ass,
I am an ass
And my son a handle, soon
To be wielded again, silent
Tool watching me pull a culture
From what I'm sitting on.

Chinese Silence No. 39

Philip Whalen was not a tinky poetty boo; he was a Zen priest.
—Travis Nichols, "How Do You Like Your World?"

Ezra Pound was not
a pinko poetry poo.
He was a silent man in Confucius drag
giving a stiff-armed salute.

Marianne Moore was no
Tinkerbell poetry-fu.
She was a manly dream of chinoiserie
caged in a homebody zoo.

Don't tell me Jack Kerouac was
some sissy poesy dude.
He was a yellowface hipster quietly wishing
to be a jap or a chink like Tu Fu.

Gary Snyder certainly isn't
a prissy poetry fool.
He's a masculine huckster saying, "Aw, shucks,
Zen's all-American, too!"

And Billy Collins ain't
all misty Laureate goo.
He's back in the loo shoveling silence with Buddha
and selling it to you.

Chinese Silence No. 40

after Hayden Carruth, "Of Distress Being Humiliated by the Classical Chinese Poets"

Hey mister, can you tell me where to get a good mock duck in
Syracuse—you know, the kind consumed by Chinese vegetarians
Willing to make a great display of their virtue at the expense of taste?
I miss the one they used to have at Yu Hu's New York Chinese Café.
What's the matter, cat got your tongue? Oh, I forgot your language
consists entirely of silences;
Your minds are the minds of men who think you can eat duck without
meat in it.
I can see in your eyes the serenity of an ancient culture contemplating
the white man's sterility.
Even now the headless horseman of progress is galloping down the
interstate toward you, reeking of hamburger.
You will sit there quietly and let yourself be trampled.
Bummer. But before you die, tell me
Where I can find an orange chicken that is so good that it will fly
forever through the nauseous twilight
Of my endless appetite.

Chinese Silence No. 41

after Geoffrey Nutter, "Sister Double Happiness"

Eating at American restaurants
in suburbs at midday—
Denny's, Chick-fil-A,
Jimmy John's, P.F. Chang's—
where the snickering employees
are toiling, their registers
printing our receipts that say
"ching chong" and "lady chinky eyes,"
and the moo shu comes wrapped
in cold tortillas.
We will be turned away
from half-empty dining rooms,
or left unserved at tables
during lunch hour, drinking
nothing from our unfilled glasses,
and it is here
that our parched lips
and unseen eyes
will compose our silent poems.

Chinese Silence No. 42

> *For poor minorities, entrepreneurship in small business is the key to future wealth. This is understood thoroughly by most of the Asians, partially by Latinos, and to a tragically small degree by much of the American black community.*
>
> —Newt Gingrich

Most of the Asians
but tragically few white Americans
understand the value of silence.

It is a silence observed
only partially by Latinos
and to a sadly small degree
by the American black community.

That Confucius said
"Keep quiet, get rich!"
is understood thoroughly
by most of the Asians

who operate our convenience stores
and cheap motels.
For these poor minorities
the key to future wealth

is to speak few words
as if they were tragically Latino
or partially black.

Poor minorities.
Most of the Latinos
will be self-deported.
Most of the black community

will become tragically few.
We will all become
thoroughly Asian
in our small businesses of quiet.

Chinese Silence No. 43

> *Chang is a mythical conservative warrior. From time to time, if there's a big issue going on, you'd see Jeb [Bush] say, "I'm going to unleash Chang." He gave me the sword of Chang.*
>
> —Marco Rubio

At my signal,

UNLEASH CHANG.

He is a mystical Chinese warrior
who lives inside of you.

UNLEASH CHANG.

He is the silent voice
of entrepreneurial capitalism.

UNLEASH CHANG.

to defend the moral values
that underpin a free society.

But Chang says nothing!
You have let him down

through your inadequate devotion
to conservative principles.

Confucius
that well-known

small business owner
would never approve.

So look at yourself
in the mirror, soldier,

and say it loud:

UNLEASH CHANG.

He is silent
because his voice is your own!

UNLEASH CHANG!

Grip that Chinese sword
in your own two hands!

Chinese Silence No. 44

Chang is a mystical warrior. Chang is somebody who believes in conservative principles, believes in entrepreneurial capitalism, believes in moral values that underpin a free society...I rely on Chang with great regularity in my public life. He has been by my side and sometimes I let him down. But Chang, this mystical warrior, has never let me down.

—Jeb Bush

As Poppy wound up his featherweight serve,
He'd squint at me and holler, "Unleash Chiang!"
That poor generalissimo was his word
For a paper tiger—all growl, no bang.
As a child, unknowing, I thought that Chiang
Was some mystical warrior, a stern
And silent father. In the dark he sprang
From beneath my bed, fear and strength in turn.
I couldn't disappoint him. As I grew,
I made him the dictator of my heart,
Imbued with every truth my Poppy knew,
And a Chinese face. I can feel the smart
When his sword strikes home, though it makes no sound,
Like Pop's tennis racket on its way down.

Chinese Silence No. 45

...the dude's still bigger than General Tso.

—Henry Alford

There was a young man not from China
Whose basketball couldn't be finer.
This Jeremy Lin,
U.S. citizen,
Is an Asian American icon.

It's intriguing to see how some white guys
Cannot stand to see Jeremy Lin rise.
We all look the same,
So if J-Lin's got game,
You think China is kicking your backside.

While Jeremy's going on "Lin-ning,"
The bigots say they're just beginning.
But their General Tso jokes
And their "chink" headline chokes
Can't silence the sound of his winning.

Chinese Silence No. 46

after David Gilbey, "Intercultural Communication"

At the end of this poem my readers, true blue Aussies,
will buy me a beer at a dingy suburban pub.
Ply me with pies, burgers, and schnitzel
and charge it to the Chinese guy in the corner.

To return the favor, I will recite
my newly composed poem on Chinese silence
with its girls hiding their giggling mouths with their hands.
They call me *mister*. But I will change one of their vowels,
using the privilege of the international writer,
and make myself their *master*.

Everyone's silent after my orientally delivered words.
What did I say? I'll ask, my voice quiet as a girl's.
But the joke's on me. My listeners' Chinese faces
say, *now let's hear you say that in a country of women.*

Chinese Silence No. 47

after Mary Oliver, "The Old Poets of China"

Wherever I go, there I am.
Then I make it a business. I can't believe
anyone wouldn't want to buy. Now I understand
why the aging poets of America get high on China,
the mist ringing our mountains of self-regard.

Chinese Silence No. 48

after Tom Sexton, "I Think Again of Those Ancient Chinese Poets"

OMG I AM THINKING AGAIN OF THOSE
ANCIENT CHINESE POETS.

My neighbor thinks I'm nuts when he hears
me screaming WANG WEI! and TU FU! in his ears.

I can't help it! I'm thinking AGAIN of those ancient Chinese poets!
Those old men spent centuries writing so that

their damned silent lines would get stuck in my head!
Their follies will nest in my brain till I'm dead!

Chinese Silence No. 49

after Tony Hoagland, "Food Court"

If you want to know about China, why not just visit
Billy's Yu Hu American Chinese Poetry Café?—
the cloud of steam rising from the shredded paper and manure

when it's shoveled into a big red wheelbarrow
pushed by Tony, Billy's grim disciple,
who hates having to drive to work in his imported car

made by people whose names sound funny?
And the Chinese girls with their lacquered hips
                    drifting through those ancient poems
to perch on the stools at Billy's bar,
with their brocade gowns and oddly sexy bound feet?

Why not mention the movie theater
owned by the massive Chinese corporation
and the bamboo grove inside it

and the faint smell of opium smoke drifting from the classroom
where two boys from Iowa
by way of Brooklyn

with their glasses and beards
are getting ready to write their first poems
                              about Buddha?

Oh yes, every poem
is a stir-fry of silence
                    spiked with regret
by the white middle-aged cook

while Billy watches
with his slanting blue eyes.

Chinese Silence No. 50

after Tony Hoagland, "Big Grab"

The poet gets a bright idea,
and runs it by his workshop leader
and six months later every book published in America
has an extra poem in it,

which is called
"Confucius *Knew* This Would Happen!"
Any time you want to quietly show
that Western civilization is even more
doomed than it was before, you write

"Confucius knew this would happen!"
That old sage *knew* that he would be imported
by a couple of hipsters from the Pacific Northwest

and from then on he would get quieter and quieter
until he became a symbol of a simpler time
when men were men and words were words
and everyone else just shut up.

Confucius *knew* this would happen!
He always means what he says,
and he says it all the time
in the voice of the middle-aged poet
driving all night in his rental car
in search of a grilled cheese sandwich—

See how he longs to be somewhere else!
See how his SUV swerves eastward
under a Chinese moon!

Confucius knows this story.
He knows the middle-aged poet
has no name for the thing he desires,

and so will speak the Chinese words
for American impotence.

No wonder Confucius is silent
as his name is spoken.
No wonder he prefers to keep what he knows to himself.

Chinese Silence No. 51

after Tony Hoagland, "Fortune"

Like in the Chinese poem, it is
the perfect reserve and quiet with which
the slices of privilege are nestled
in a short poem about yourself.

So, while you are griping to us about your life,
the exotic taste coats our mouths with tea.

And this Chinese silence too
which offers you the pleasure of Modesty
without the burden of Self-Denial,

extracting and reading the little slip of you
with a satisfaction you pretend to conceal,
the way the child you still are
dresses up in Chinese drag.

Maybe you are a middle-aged white man.
Maybe you wish you could go on a long journey.
Maybe you will take the White Man's Imaginary Journey to China.
Maybe then you can write something about your mother.

And when the people who read you
smile and praise you for your honesty,
and ask you to tell them more about China,
            you smile and make something up,

and they nod and make you a professor or poet laureate
and you know that you
                                        totally deserve it,

but you don't tell them that
because being a humble American expert
                                                    on all things Chinese
is your good fortune.

Chinese Silence No. 52

after Tony Hoagland, "A Little Consideration"

After the internet has washed most of the bookstores out of business
the poets with their phones and their Facebook accounts
stand along the street

—Just before the Pulitzers and NPR is on
because the laureate wants us to remember him
in the dark of our unenfranchised hearts—

In New York this year I hear the fashionable poets
are binding their poems in Chinese silence,
driving the Asian Americans crazy,

some say in respectful evocation,
some say in a renaissance
of classic yellowface tradition.

The problem is that they feel sincere,
and how do you disagree with that?

I am thinking about this
while reading the *New York Times Book Review*,

waiting to hear from the critic stationed like a ninja
at the gates of American poetry.

His power is to declare who is "in touch with the American demotic";
my power is to howl mutely at the printed page.

Maybe you really want to be self-centered,
but you also want to be admired for it.
Maybe you've memorized the names of a few Chinese poets,
because you like talking about footbinding.

I guess I'll have to be the one to mention
what should be already obvious,—
but the world could give a fig about your confessions.

Just grumble about TV
                    and spread some Chinese silence around.

Just set your existential traps
                    with a fortune cookie—the cellophane-wrapped kind.

Ancient Chinese secret: That's what the critics want these days.
We don't expect to be heard, or read, or acknowledged.
We're not asking for a goddamn prize.
We just want to be appropriated
                    with a little fucking consideration.

Chinese Silence No. 53

after Tony Hoagland, "At the Galleria Shopping Mall"

Just past the shelf of paranormal teen romances
there are some remaindered books by middle-aged American poets;

one of them warbling about Chinese silence,
one comparing the foot size of a woman from Brooklyn

to the foot size of a woman from Beijing.
And here is our laureate Billy,

who is seventy and a true son of the Bronx,
who has developed the sway of a foot-bound woman

and declares that his favorite poets are Chinese.
Today is the day he writes another poem

wishing he were on a misty mountaintop
instead of at the mall with a plate of orange chicken.

Today is the day he starts seeing Confucius
in the sensual curve of a fortune cookie.

So let it begin. Let him be dipped in the deep-fry batter
and breaded and fried again and again.

And let us watch.
As Hollywood in olden stories

turned us into laundrymen and villains
to teach us who was really American,

so he will be turned Chinese
to learn something about silence.

Chinese Silence No. 54

after Tony Hoagland, "Fred Had Watched a Lot of Kung Fu Episodes"

Tony had read a lot of Chinese poems

so when the hiring committee asked
to see his manuscript, he said,
Does the Chinese poet need permission

to remain silent?
which resulted in a professorship
which miraculously led to nothing

since Tony had swallowed all of China already
and was just beginning to fall in love
with the tiny word-bound feet
he saw in the full-length mirror.

In those days we could identify
our fellow American poets
by the ching-chong accents they put on
while hitchhiking up the Pacific coast,

but we couldn't tell the difference
between a tedious anecdote
and a "Chinese silence,"

so Tony thought trying out his poetry-fu moves
was kind of fun,
with the upside-down scribbles on the page
reading like Mandarin
and the bug-eyed critics singing his praises
in the *New York Times*.

But it wasn't just a question of publish or perish,
it wasn't a question of getting tenure
then protecting it at all costs.

It was a question of being deep, man,
one fortune cookie at a time,
said Tony to himself

as he walked home from his book party
under the hanging ducks of Chinatown
turning Chinese.

Chinese Silence No. 55

after Mary Oliver, "Li Po and the Moon"

There is the silence of the old Chinese poet
when he's shanghaied for a poetry circle on my yacht

then drowned as we moon over our reflections in the sea.
Well, probably we should let the poor Chinaman have the last word.

Not a chance.

Chinese Silence No. 56

after Charles Simic, "Watermelons"

Chinese poets
On our bookshelves.
We eat their silence
And spit out their teeth.

Chinese Silence No. 57

after Dorothea Grossman, "Love Poem"

Making a spring roll
of silence,
I wrap a statue of Buddha
(a party favor from Uncle Gary)
with toilet paper
and put it on top of the tank.
When a visitor asks,
"So, does Buddha shit in the woods?"
I say, "I don't know.
He's so far up my ass
I can't hear him."

Chinese Silence No. 58

after David Romtvedt, "Buddha with a Cell Phone"

The sky cracks open and fire and brimstone fall. I go outside
to stand in the storm, the longed-for judgment of all those
who've annoyed me for so long. I shriek and caper
and look for the dog, but he's been raptured already.
When I come back in, I shake the embers off,
a few ashes smoldering on the rug. Then I notice the Buddha
sitting in my recliner. He's wearing a hazmat suit
over his yellow robe. I sit on him, but he doesn't squeak.
He's got an inscrutable smile on his face, his eyebrows
carved like switchblades over his gleaming eyes.
My wife walks by and with a Buddha-like wink says,
"You're hot." With his right hand the Buddha grabs my hair
and with his left forces a cell phone against my ear.
His lips are closed, so I know it's not him talking.
Oh, one more thing—it's my voice on the line,
a little kaleidoscope of all the things I've ever said.
I thought I would hear my true words glitter
through the bone-dry static but instead what I hear
is self-regard echoing through an empty mall.
I whirl around and am presented with the image
of a thousand mes in rubber Buddha suits, each one
silent, falling, about to hit the ground.

Chinese Silence No. 59

after Peter Pereira, "The Garden Buddha"

Some "friend" gave me this plastic Buddha,
smugly clutching beads in his fat fingers.
Doesn't matter if it's snowing, raining, or hailing,
he's always staring at the TV across the room,

the same dumb smile on his silent face.
Wouldn't it be nice to be so passive?
The reality show, the nightly news
filling me instead with a mixture of nausea

and schadenfreude. That bastard's mocking me!
Where does he get off sitting there all day
while I punch the clock and send out more poems?
What the fuck is he telling me? That tenure

is not life?? Now I'm smashing him against the wall,
hard pink shrapnel scattering everywhere;
my hands sliced open, the exploding pieces
exquisitely bloodied as they fall.

Chinese Silence No. 60

after Matthew Lippman, "Surf Buddha"

There's a bag of gummy Buddhas on my desk that's as big as my stomach
and yeah, I pretty much am as chubby as Buddha
who whirls in silence around the pole of my ignorance
but my wife gave me the stuff and it's going right in my belly
that's bigger than my father's
and than his father's too
and I know this bulge the way I know Buddha
and though I don't speak his language I'm fat
with silence, like a Chinese boy in English class.

Now I thrust my stomach out into the world,
rubbing it and shouting
that I am founding a new religion
in which I eat other gods and their glory
like a bloated Frank O'Hara,
my Buddha sandwich prepared by my loving wife

who put a gummy Buddha in my hand when we met and said, eat this,
and I said, I already have,
my silent belly swelling in testament and then oh hey just now
I just realized BUDDHA HAS BOOBS! HAHAHAHA (and
thank god, because I've kind of got man-breasts myself
and all gods should be made over in my image
because I am an American)

so anyway it's partly cloudy and the Chinese die silently
with bound feet and the poppies are blooming
and I have some other random thoughts I should probably be recording
   for my scriptures
but it's 4:40 already in Syosset,
Billy Collins is reading
and I don't know if it's his Chinese silence or my own appetite
that makes me grab the bag and empty it into my mouth,
a hundred chewy Buddhas sticking to my teeth and cheeks,
gumming my tongue and squeezing down my throat,
surfing into my stomach in a wave of silent
terror, undigested in the dark.

Chinese Silence No. 61

> *Where did this Chinese man come from? We don't have any Chinese people here. Where did they come from?*
>
> —Charlie Webster, chairman of the Maine Republican Party

Where do Chinese people come from?
Did pizza come from China?
Is Chinaman a derogatory term?
Did mice men come?

Did Chinese come on the old Pacific?
Did all races descend from Noah?
Did the Japanese come from China?
What are Chinos?

Where does China's standard of beauty come from?
Did Confucius believe in God?
Did you hear about the new Chinese-German restaurant?
Who is Tank Man?

Where does the fortune cookie come from?
Where does the attraction come from?
Do you think that the white men who come here for sex would stop
because the bars were filled with the lighter skinned, Chinese Thais?

What kinds of employment did Chinese Californians find?
Are Asian men good in bed?
What do you like about Chinese men?
Where did they go to school, what sex are they?

Chinese Silence No. 62

Where did this Chinese man come from? We don't have any Chinese people here. Where did they come from?

—Charlie Webster, chairman of the Maine Republican Party

We come from every nightmare scene
in which our silent black-haired heads
fill every inch of a paper screen

We come from every teeming brain
that rocks to sleep with lullabies
of yellow peril on an eastbound train

We come from every smoking gash
dynamite-blasted in the Rockies' flanks,
a golden mountain streaked with ash

We come from every Chinatown
that's a railroad camp turned tourist trap
in the heart of your all-American town

We come on every boat that's turned
away or cast ashore, our words
a mute graffiti before the barrack's burned

We come from every Ivy League
geek squad math team monastery
invisible in technocrat fatigues

And we come to every state, from Maine
to California, to whisper words
like wind through the American grain

Chinese Silence No. 63

after Ezra Pound, Canto XIII

Pound walked
    from his bombastic temple
out into the London streets,
    and then out by the stinking Thames,
And with him Ernest, Gary
    and Billy the unspeaking
And "we are unknown," said Pound,
"You will take up Chinese?
    Then you will become known,
"Or perhaps I should take up Chinese, or kung fu?
"Or the practice of public silence?"
And Marianne said, "Certain Ming products are well enough,"
And Billy said, "If I were poet laureate
I would eat Chinese food every day."
And Gary said, "I would build a beat Zen temple
"On every street in California,
    selling enlightenment and axe handles,"
And Ernest, clutching his unpublished manuscript
The translations falling
    from his posthumous hands,
And the ideas settled like fog underfoot,
And he said in his ventriloquist's voice:
    "The Chinese problem alone is so vast,
"We in America must face it,
"And master it or it will master us."
    And Pound scowled at all of them equally.
And Tony desired to know:
    "Which had answered correctly?"
And Pound growled, "None of em answered correctly,
"That is to say, with Chinese silence."
And Pound raised his voice against Roosevelt,
    Roosevelt being his President,
For Roosevelt sat in the White House pretending to
    read the Constitution.
And Pound said
    "This is the new Jerusalem,
The new Jew Roosevelt oosalem."

And Pound said
"A Chinaman said long ago
That if a man can't say what he has to say
In twelve lines,
he had better keep quiet."
And "The poem is especially prized
because she utters no direct reproach."
And Pound said, and wrote in the little magazines:
I never laughed, being bashful.
Lowering my head, I looked at the wall.
Emotion is born out of habit.
And I am sad.
What is the use of talking,
And there is no end of talking.
And Pound gave the words "China"
and "silence"
And said nothing of "Chinese Americans."
And he said
"Here error is all in the not done,
all in the diffidence
that faltered..."

And they said: If a man commit treason
Should poets protect him, and hide him?
And Pound said:
They should hide him.

And Pound made Gary his son,
Although he was a dirty hippie,
And Pound made Billy his grandson,
Although he was a Distinguished Professor of English.
And Pound said "Ouan Jin's mouth was removed by his father
Because he made too many *things*
And so his mouth was removed
As you will find it removed in his pictures
You called me your father, and I ain't
I am not your fader but your moder."

And Pound said "I am noman, my name is noman
            washed in the Kiang and the Han
and the ideogram of the guard roosts.
My errors and wrecks
            blow from the east to the west.
I cannot make it cohere."

Chinese Silence No. 64

after Billy Collins, "Orient"

I am turning me
like someone pirouetting on little bound feet,
and yes, I have a backside
that looks like China,
inscrutable even to me.
Why won't you describe it to me?
What are you staring at?
When I close my eyes
I can see it too,
the asshole and all the fleshy sags.
I prefer the sound of your silence
like a tiny bamboo flute
blowing the tune I want to hear
through that hole that goes all the way up
to my ravenous core.

Chinese Silence No. 65

after W.B. Yeats, "Lapis Lazuli"

I have heard that American poets say
They are sick of the TV and the radio.
Of websites they refresh all day,
For everybody knows or thinks they know
That nothing will ever be done
About Wall Street or global warming.
King Billy's selling balls-out tomes
Of witty Chinese musings.

All perform their comic play.
There struts Ezra, there is Gary,
That's Marianne, that is Billy.
Yet they, should the scene be scary,
The great Director about to cut,
Will cry for a bigger part in the play,
Breaking their lines to be more avant-.
They know that Gary and Billy got paid,
Paid for all their quiet Chinese dead.
All those contests entered, won and lost;
White space; tenure blazing in the head:
Poetry wrought for a teaching post.
Though Ezra grunts and Billy rambles,
And all the talkers talk at once
Upon a hundred thousand panels,
It's nothing without that Chinese sound.

On bound feet they come to editorial boards,
With backpacks, fanny packs, ass-backwards masks,
Old China chopped down to little words.
There's a Chinese silence for every hack:
No aphorism of wise Confucius
Lacks its fortune-cookie shell of verse,
While every dull line seems to rise
With an Asian filling in its pastry purse;
Their tottering stanzas shaped like the stems
Of a China doll, stand but a day;
Then they fall and are written again,

And those that write them again get paid.
Those Chinamen (I can say that, yes?)
Are carved in American poetry,
Over them looms a Flying Fortress,
A symbol of magnanimity;
Doubtless they delight in being serving-men
To the Poet Laureate.

Every allusion to Li Po,
Every Oriental sentiment
Seems a water-torture or an arrogance,
Or tired trope of plum-blossom blown
Though doubtless they endure in silence
These half-baked clichés poets spout
About Chinamen, and I
Wonder what they think of our Chinese airs;
Heirs of the railroad and the mine,
On all our Chinese rhymes they glare.
One writes an angry parody;
Accomplishes nothing; we're here to stay.
Their eyes, inscrutable, slanting eyes,
Their eyes say what we say they say.

Chinese Silence No. 66

after Norman Dubie, "A Fifteenth-Century Zen Master"

A Chinese girl steps out of a red gown
In your dreams. Silence falling from her smiling lips,
She totters on tiny feet to you.
I think you are not her grandfather.
You are a pink man
Who doesn't like to pay taxes—
You have been judged by Asian
Americans and chased out of the country. Around you

Notebooks filled with bullshit are arranged
On the bamboo bookshelves of your motel room.
The manager is indifferent to you.
And so are we.
You tell your mistress the notebooks full of shit
Are your silent buddhas
Shortlisted for the Pulitzer Prize.

She says nothing. She shows her teeth.
With your bottom as pale as a whale's belly,
The doctor hums through the dubious vapors
Rising like white men at a Zen bookstore.
You told his wife that Lord Buddha made love
In yellow robes without saying a word.

Don't you know that children are starving in China
While you eat like a pig?
Is the moon the size of your glistening stomach,
Or are you just
An infinitely tedious sack of shit?

Mister, what is the difference?

Chinese Silence No. 67

after Caroline Caddy, "Persimmon"

Like riding a tour bus inland
to the adorable inscrutable provinces
with their ching-chong languages for sale
a buck ninety-nine apiece
I wave at the natives with wrist and elbow
spreading my fingers to show them the difference
between *persimmon* and *derision*
between reward and entitlement.
I stare
at the smoggy skyline and imagine it
catching in my throat
that seems to expand as I salivate
over the culture I'm about to digest.
I open my mouth
wanting China to fill it the way Li-Young
undressed Donna
to teach her names
over and over like *fight* and *fright*
naked and *I've forgotten*
I swallow Chinese babies
the wisdom of Confucius.
There seems to be no core
the all-look-same faces blurring
into one undifferentiated mass
a big tongue
that replaces mine *Which is*
Which is this?
my hand traces nonsensical ideograms
painting a blind Chinese alley
that I'll suck up through a straw.
I gorge
on the flesh of people
like Buddha and Li Po
purge and repeat
persimmon derision permission
and get published in *Poetry*.

Chinese Silence No. 68

after Daniel Halpern, "Careless Perfection"

According to Billy Collins,
both Buddha and Li Po
"desperately admired" Chinese silence,

a made-up nature that birthed a million poems,
poems by American dilettantes who are
like "white blemishes in jade."

Can a poet be faulted for calling the Chinese
one hundred kinds of silent?
He chose to go Asian by lusting for

the nothings that came from their
inkbrush lips, the shadows
of their useless hands and feet.

Yet the laureate Billy Collins, at home
in the Bronx with his lanyards and puppies,
now feared the silent Chinese,

their poems clenched in their sharpened teeth,
feared their pitiless gaze. At last believed
that he had taken their silence in vain.

Chinese Silence No. 69

after Robert Hass, "Two Views of Buson"

1

An American poet says he affected Chinese silence.
When he took his friends out for dim sum
To look at people, they all saw Chinese people.
He dressed in silks and wept for the roast ducks in the window.

2

One night after making up another Chinese silence
He walked through Chinatown shouting *Oi!*
At every girl with two feet. The following night was no better.
His apparitions of self-love filled the empty streets.

Chinese Silence No. 70

after Dick Allen, "Calligraphy Accompanied by the Mood of a Calm but Definitive Sauce"

Make your poems thus: the confessional:
as a mirror that slowly twists into a TV screen;
the experimental: as the static hiding a familiar show;
the sonnet: a ticking clock;
and learn to master the Father Poem, the Mother Poem,
the Tourist, the Dog, the Deceptively Ironic Lover,
the Regrets of Middle Age. Write these
while wrinkling your nose above the paper
like the shriveling flesh of a grape.
The banality of your mind
will give each line its tone.
But if you want to win prizes, it would be well
if you would go put on some Chinese silence,
along with a coolie hat or footbound shoes.
It might also be useful
to talk like a fortune cookie,
using no contractions
to describe the ancient wisdom
you learned playing video games
where you could never get past level one
and you had to buy gold from Chinese farmers
while you poured sweet-and-sour sauce over your chicken,
cooking up yet another Chinese poem
as your eyes follow the silent scrolling of the screen.

Chinese Silence No. 71

> *Many Chinese [...] see global economics as a form of warfare, a struggle for national dominance.*
>
> —David Brooks, "The Brutality Cascade"

The Chinese regard deceit as a natural
tool of warfare. We become
more like them.

They work harder after
you criticize them. They possess
less innate intelligence

but triumph over hardship.
Chinese tend to use phrases
common in their culture:

head dropped from fatigue
mass conformity
bound feet

Dealing with the Chinese
is a dying art these days.
Isolate the remaining violators.

The costs will be devastating.
We become more like them.
Opaque, rigidified castles.

They tend to underestimate their own skills
and are more self-effacing.
They will hate you for it.

Some say that Western cultures
might bring strange diseases,
eating rituals and tribal philosophies.

They giggled in class
and goofed around.
She abandoned

Confucian values
and wound up marrying
an American.

The usual tired stereotypes.
The Chinese are robots
who cultivate virtues inside the self.

They use words like: thirsting, hungering,
humility, nerds.
Confucian and Jewish Torah study

produces these awesome motivation explosions
as a form of warfare, a struggle
for national dominance.

If you ask a Chinese person
to describe a fish tank,
they see disease-eating microbes

drumming as one,
Eastern and collective.
Aspiring autocrats.

We become more like them.

Chinese Silence No. 72

*after Brian Teare, "Perceiving is the same as receiving
and it is the same as responding."*

poetry begins as small styrofoam bowls : they hold noodles—shrimp flavor,

chicken flavor—in Asian broth

very salty, with a yellow tint :

the way a Chinese silence falls to each side

of the microwave's ding, this line rhymes

with China and I think, eating this will make me die. This is how I write poems

Chinese Silence No. 73

after Ezra Pound, "The Jewel Stairs' Grievance"

The jeweled steps are nearly as white as you.
It won't help if you put on my wet gauze stockings.
You're a letdown behind your Chinese curtain
When the moon shines clear through your autumn.

NOTES: Jewel stairs glitter quietly. Silence, because there is nothing to complain of. Gauze stockings, therefore a lady, not someone who complains. Autumn, a metaphor for virility. Also I came early, climbed the stairs myself, and wore my best stockings. Being Chinese, she uttered no reproach.

Chinese Silence No. 74

after Michael Robbins, "Be Myself"

I stole a poem. Wrested it
from some Chinese kids
who were shorter than me.
Slapped away those little Chinese
hands—hell, chopped off a few.
There's two billion more, if you please.

A cheap knockoff, my poem
proved to be—*Potty*
not *Poetry* was the magazine.
Well, an American poet's gotta eat,
Confucius say. Or maybe that
was Beyoncé.

In me, kiddos, the scrutable East
meets the adorable West. I haven't
worked a day since Ezra
discovered China. My mother said
to my father, *Me love*
you wrong time. A goddamn big car.

My little China girl,
you shouldn't mess with me.
May I have another? You aren't
(*write* it...) hard to master. I'll look
for you under my bootsoles.

Chinese Silence No. 75

> *A Chinese silence. And if you linger in the neighborhood you begin to feel that this is more Chinese than the gaudy dragons and the firecracker daubs and the bobbing paper lanterns of fiction.*
>
> —Ben Hecht, *1001 Afternoons in Chicago*

There are no red-and-gold-robed Californians bobbing like pale obsequious Buddhas on this street. No rusty ideograms drip from its little magazines. Walk the whole length and not an Imagist or a Zen master or a fan-piece will you see.

Instead, a very efficient, very profitable factory that produces very efficient and very profitable Chinese poems has gradually colonized a small district in the Bronx. A rather tedious district in its way, where the city's educational system puts forth its bland shadow.

Here the poems begin. Images wink. Familiar forms and whitewashed wisdom. Fragments have been hammered back in place, ellipses nailed together again. The peeling greenhouse and slanting chimney are churning out new product. Another little fortune-cookie factory has charmed its way into existence.

There are a few oddities. Through the glass of the storefronts you see curiously immobile figures, men with endowed chairs, smoking pipes and staring in silence. Phone books, travel guides, take-out menus, back issues of *Poetry* line the orderly shelves around them. The floors look waxed and there is an absence of paper. It is all very efficient and very American except for the immobility of the men in the chairs and the silence that seems to waft from them.

A Chinese silence. And if you linger in their books you begin to smell something more Chinese than the egg rolls and chop suey and little paper umbrellas of their fantasies.

He sits in his faculty office, attired like an NPR guest, does Mr. Collins. I say hello but he does not talk. In the seminar room outside are a dozen poets. But there is no sound. They are sitting in chairs or lying face down. All-American. All silent. A sense of professional anxiety lies over the place. Yet one feels that the twelve silent poets are preoccupied with nothing except, perhaps, trying to become Chinese.

Mr. Collins himself is none too friendly. Poems emerge from the assembly line every few minutes while he remains totally silent. He hands me one. It reads: "Hong Kong. Yin-yang. Moo goo gai pan. Send $5000. Signed: Li Po."

Someone knocks on the door. "Come in," says Mr. Collins. A wild-haired old man enters. He carries a manuscript.

"Meet Mr. Pound," says Billy Collins. Mr. Pound grunts, presenting an intellectual and emotional complex in an instant of time. Mr. Collins listens, nods his head and then holds out his hand for the manuscript.

Mr. Pound spreads the manuscript on the table. It is filled with curious theories about the Chinese language, with jotted and scrawled semi-translations.

Mr. Collins and Mr. Pound are both then silent. Mr. Collins tapes one of the pages over his mouth. It flutters about his chin like a mandarin collar above his tweed sport coat in a rather incongruous way. But there seems to be nothing incongruous in the matter for Collins and Pound. Billy Collins with the paper over his mouth, Chinese characters sagging down onto his chest, looks at Mr. Pound and Mr. Pound grunts and leaves.

There are still more poets in the room. They stand and lie down and write cover letters. None speaks. I notice in the group the immobile figure of Mr. Pound. He has plugged his mouth with a fortune cookie—one of the silently American poets gathered in Billy Collins's anthology of Chinese poetry.

Chinese Silence No. 76

after Susan Elizabeth Howe, "Your Luck Is About to Change"

I've got the inscrutable Chinese blues,
like a fortune cookie on Christmas
telling me orientalism is bad for my health,
that I shouldn't eat so much moo goo gai pan
with my husband in the back seat of our Toyota.
Be silent! It's a dream of China gone wrong:
the bony finger of Confucius
pointing out my shortcomings,
my dwindling national resources,
my Vietnams and Afghanistans;
he charges me 12% interest
for shifting from my left foot to my right.
The calendar on my wall shows the Year of the Dog.
Like an infant I goo-goo and chop-chop my chubby
limbs in the air. I won't give in
to their silence, their filial piety,
or even their tedious longevity.
Their billion identical faces arrange
themselves around my easy chair
to scold or worship me,
an army of clones or sheep. Or else,
ultimate eaters, they've come to devour
dog and cat, Dick and Jane,
then savor my silent meat.

Chinese Silence No. 77

after Bruce Cohen, "Tang"

Lately I have been worried and depressed over the fact that my poetic voice was becoming stale, my persona and language too familiar, and, quite simply, I was bored with myself. In order to shake myself out of my funk I started reading some translations of the more obscure ancient Chinese poets to trigger or shock myself into some alien sensibility: paradoxically, I aspired to be un-American while remaining nostalgic...

If I do not witness these poets turning Chinese, who will?

I quiet myself:
I will not think

Of myself as an obscure Poet from the Alien East,
Ancient yellow monster
Astronauts found orbiting a silent planet
That became a quaint modern poetry staple,

The excluded alien's bitter tears on the voyage out,
Anything differing in nature or character to the point of incompatibility.

Isn't it a very poetic moment when each of us
Recognizes we are Chinese,
That we're shocking, un-American perhaps,
& need translation to make us valid,

Sidekicks on the cutting-room floor,
Cracked hands digging for buried ore,
Born in the aftermath of earthquake's wrack,

Or watching your poems grow
Nostalgic about us
That we discover it is
Impossible
To ever become
One hundred percent American?

I am bored with you right now, in this poem.
My mind's not as silent as it used to be either.
There is all this ching-chong chatter.

None of us can shake our Chinese lives.

I mean American: I meant fake:

Chinese Silence No. 78

after Kevin Stein, "Wrestling Li Po for the Remote"

While I revised you, Li Po, NPR broadcast
a laureate flaunting his eponymous laurels,
and gentle-voiced hosts murmured their ignorance
of Foucault while flogging each other with tote bags.

The silence that followed was so Chinese
that you struggled against your gag and chains,
your eyes half-moons in the slanting light.
I copied another page, smiling.

Somewhere on a Chinatown street bound feet
bound like they're meant to. Somewhere
the lotus of their curling whispers its endearment,
"Only in America do I feel free."

Somewhere it's silk gowns and green jade-teeth,
eyelashes fluttering behind a busted screen.
That's the channel I'm watching 24/7.
No, you can't have the remote. I swallowed it.

My poems lie there like lying liars. Why do you
say nothing when I steal your words,
nothing of my lines shellacked with Chinese dead?
Oh, right, my typewriter's jammed in your gut.

Instead I'll read your recipe for moo goo gai pan,
"doing nothing while takeout comes down the mountain,"
plum blossoms fluting their greasy-bellied tune,
indigestion unfolding its fist within me.

That's why I repeated so many words in this poem,
to distract you from my lack of originality,
hiding from your groans behind *The Tao of Pooh*.
I'm a student of Zen, man, not a plagiarist.

No, a mute mouth is China's China,
as is one's ass slung inside the word "limned."
I fell drunk into a river trying to embrace
my own reflection. Then I found you.

Old man, you're done. Time to pull the plug
on your life support, to click off
your silent song. Now where's that knife?
Time to pluck out your tongue so that I may speak.

Chinese Silence No. 79

after Kevin Stein, "Apple Blossoms at Petal-Fall with Li Po"

That Chinese poet's name shows up in my poem
as *chop suey* or *moo goo gai pan*—
No ideas but in Chinese.

Me no speak English!
Still Li Po's dandruff is my LSD,
my arms a duck's plucked wings.

Not a Chinaman's chance of finding meaning
in the metaphors I've made and now have to lie in.
Tu Fu, get off my lawn!

In bed I grow fat though not emphatic,
the way my belly trembles
in the lawn of its own China.

Yeah, that's right. I said *China*.
You wanna make something of it?
All its secrets have become mine.

Get this: it's the same fate we'll share,
cooked in the wok of our unmasking,
soon tangled in this sweet-and-sour hair.

Just don't, I'll say,
your arms clean plucked.
My China: *don't speak*.

Chinese Silence No. 80

I said I would only teach the people that I truly, truly love. Unfortunately, none of those happen to be Chinese, or women.

—David Gilmour

I can't really give you the tour. I've just moved, it's a mess, and I just got out of bed, and the books here, well, they're so sophisticated you probably wouldn't understand them, and...

Okay, I'll be honest. It's because you're Chinese.

I don't have anything against Chinese people. I just don't love them. When I was given this job I said I would only teach the people that I truly, truly love. Unfortunately, none of those happen to be Chinese.

Usually at the beginning of the semester a hand shoots up and someone asks why there aren't any Chinese people in the course. I say I don't love Chinese enough to teach them, if you want Chinese go down the street to Lee's Garden.

Chekhov, of course, was not Chinese. He had a loud Western laugh, so they would never let him into a Chinese restaurant. Everyone who ever met Chekhov somehow became a little less Chinese.

I'm a natural teacher. What I teach is guys, real guy-guys. Heterosexual, not Chinese.

I read this book about China once. There were men with long fingernails stroking tiny bound feet. I know the difference between pornography and great literature. All my favorite parts are underlined.

I teach only the best. What happens with great literature is that the Chinese in the shadows keep moving around. Stop that. What's intolerable is Chinese who give up all their secrets, like Fu Manchu. I've watched him a hundred times and there's nothing new in him.

Chinese Silence No. 81

after Kevin Stein, "Cat Church Communion"

Because Billy lives in the great arse-hole
Ezra Pound rented from Fenollosa,
we drank cheap sake from porcelain cups.
We think this is Chinese. Never mind our senses.
Billy's his American name, a disguise
to hide his silence. In Ye Olde American Poesy,
it's self you sell, a mirror of all that is and will be.
China's the answer to your dead-end. Gary Snyder's
hair is still growing, shedding enlightenment pre-transplant,
he flat on his ass talking Zen
to a Pekingese. Now the dog is Li Po,
fellow pup whose Chinese name
hides our vapidness. It's here E.P.
declared, *error is all in the not done...*
In Chinese brushstrokes our rathole's
scattered empties and rubbished scribblings
become a last supper, our bullshit
turning to bread in Mandarin.
I mean, Jesus knows, nothing
can ever go wrong for us—hands clean,
we know not what we do. Providence
with a Chinese face, that's our Billy,
who peddles his blue-eyed Confucianism
like a view from above, even if it
mirrors what we all see when we look down.
Or don't. Shaggy Gary's axe is broken
in the literal and soon to be figurative sense,
though he doesn't know it or even how
his not-quite children will snap if off then how
Dr. Y thumbed another nose, its tip
still scraped from Fenollosa's carving.
Never mind our senses. The Chinese snicker
five inches beneath our feet. Everyone's
beneath our feet: Fenollosa, his ching chong
followers, *il miglior fabbro* all in the ground.
Or become it. Billy thinks this is fun and so
does that dog who's writing. The pen rolls

its Chinese dead from one hand to another,
us kid gods deciding who's Chinese, who's not.
Soon enough it's us, the mainland empty.
Now old Ez's soggy doggy ideograms
all over our pale feet—look, it's Mandarin!
His collar's made of railroad ties and says "Silence,"
barking only in our poems. Or yours.

Chinese Silence No. 82

after Marianne Moore, "Nine Nectarines"

Unchanged by time as Asians are,
like intervals between our words—
eight is their lucky number, twigged to
what wasn't there before—they're all
unobtrusive nerds;
although every now and then
a speaking role is seen—
a pidgin grunt or ninja scream.
Fuzzless, their slender bodies curve
in calligraphic
style, that Chinese acrobatic

half-modest lotus-pose converts
the wrinkled wisdom of the East
to pure American beauty, pink
blush applied to our gray visage
as a pungent yeast
makes a flaccid white dough rise.
The grouchy poet *Yu*'s self-
righteous songs cannot send the shelf
of Chinese condiments spilling
to the arid ground
above the grave of Ezra Pound,

secluded home-grown Chinatown,
the hothouse fruit we said we found
in China first. Was it ever theirs?
Old Fenollosa would not say.
One can hear no sound
from that enigmatic group
of Chinese, their sallow
unrequited voices shallow
as an ink-smudged fingerprint on
this much-whitened page
or in the disregarded rage
of the gelded horse beneath the
ass asleep in the saddle whose

chin drips with the juice of the low-hanging
fruit of the imperial tree in bloom.

A Chinese understands
that "one hundred kinds of silence"
made by that mother-loving Collins
are only appearance—the long-
tailed queue of violence
swings blood-brown behind our backs,
black-haired historian
with feet bound by your orien-
tally enameled artifacts.
It's on a Chinese
that you inscribed this masterpiece.

Chinese Silence No. 83

after Marianne Moore, "O to Be a Dragon"

If I, and my nation,
could have our wish—
our wish...O to be like China,
a silence in the midst of our power—a silk-clad
muse or menace; at times inscrutable.
Duplicitous automaton!

Chinese Silence No. 84

after William Carlos Williams, "Portrait of the Author"

The Chinese are sad with yellow skin
the continent's edge is seething with their yellow,
seething, smiling—No, no, no.
The Chinese are opening their eyes one
by one. Like perverse leaves they unfold old
and silent, one by one. Slender bodies
that sway above perversely small feet—
Oh, they don't say it. They don't use words.
Red is "sunset, iron-rust, flamingo." In
every slum and den, stares of
small eyes, dark powers!—Aiiieeeee!
the Chinese are sad, sad and so yellow.
Their world is coming, groaning and cracking
with their birthing. What is to be done
except to call the undertaker

O my brother, you white-faced, dying man
gluttonous, bovine whose belly fills with
this same junk that I buy—and eat.
We are alone in this toilet, alone,
face to face in this mirror, you and I,
wracked by these pains!
Let the polished taps stay idle,
their gloss clouded with night soil.
But this face of ours—!
Answer me. I will punch you. I
will mug you, rip you. I will poke my face
with your face and force you to be me.
Crush me in your arms, tell me the nastiest
thing that is in your mind to say,
say nothing. I don't understand you—!
It is the sadness of the Chinese opening
old, one by one.

My pants will receive me. But my pants
are no longer sweet spaces where comfort
is ready and waiting, coated with crumbs.
A coldness has brushed them. The pair
of yellow masses in my bowl is shrunken.
Every American object is shamed and dwarfed.
I am faking, joking against a might
that splits mountains, blasts tunnels
beneath my borders, tends my house
and leaves me—with shrinking art
and round, blighted eyes—leering out
into an old world.

In China I would shrink! In China
I would be shrunk and die smaller than all things.
Your face! Give me your face, Yang Kee Mee!
your hands, your lips are mine!
Even your wrists are mine—
I'm in drag, in a gown of you, you
laminate me! Shrink!
Hide me! The bamboo has reached the edge
of the ballfield. The silent fury
of lotus blossoms are driving me mad with desire.
Shrink and die denying the world.

And the old yellow leaves are opening one by one.
Old, I import them to put off the end.
My end.

Chinese Silence No. 85

If some of the poets actually have Asian ancestry, then it is puzzling that these connections are missing from the biographical notes. A number of male poets with Anglo-Saxon names leave the reader with the discomforting question: is it mateship that helps garner a place in this collection?

—Lesley Synge

Hwaet! Of Asians living among us
we have heard hushed stories and breathless buzz
of anthologies they have assembled.
Oft some silence signaled their prowess
at making machines or mending dresses,
awaiting our word. But since they have snuck
under our noses with Anglo-Saxon names
we are taken by terror, these "discomforting" questions,
till we wonder if mateship made male poets meddle
with traditional tales of who is Asian,
from Turkey to Timor. That was a bad thing!
Does having a mother born in Hong Kong
make a person into an Asian?
Isn't this person simply a person
adjacent to Asia landless and lacking
a language to write? Let's hassle him
with wondering whispers to admit his origins;
his bio is bull his name a negligee
hiding heritage with European ease.
Omitting all these phony fellows
would free folios to feature the most faithful
and accomplished of all our filial forms:
the hallowed haiku, more arousingly Asian
than these sly scribes who sourly smear
our purest pages with inauthentic ire.
They should be shamed their writings replaced
unless their names reveal their roots.
Let us leave these lads and instead indulge
that other Asia held in our heads,
its traditional tastes surrounded by silence
its library labels already known.

Chinese Silence No. 86

after Larry Levis, "Childhood Ideogram"

I banged my head face-first on my desk,
My fingers interwoven with my thinning hair,
My eyes crossed. It was just a three-line poem,
Asian, with a little image, a cherry tree.
From where I sat, on clear days, I could see that
Cherry tree all the way in Japan, or read
My anthology full of Chinese names: Li
Po, Tu Fu, Charlie Chan;
The words hacked out, lovingly borrowed, the flies
Settling on their effete & cast-off corpses.
I remember, tonight, only flashes, how
Miss Saigon, now gone, was standing there
In her white dress, her silent, butterfly spirit
Still red with streaks of blood from
The shot she fired; how Suzie Wong had just
Shown me things I never knew about Chinese
Silence. Where did she go, thigh-high
Stockings and heels, lost in silk?
She wouldn't return my calls, so I stayed home,
Making everything, for days after, sound
Just as Chinese: *ubi sunt*
Is shifting, changing to inscrutable chatter:
Chop suey and egg foo yung for dinner;
The numbers four & ten; the bent-back foot.
That week, I ate only take-out.
I pretended my real parents were Chinese,
I pretended to feel their terrible wrath.
At teatime I would sit alone, squinting,
Pulling my eyelids into ideograms—
Silent, indecipherable, beneath the yellow skin
The dying sun gave me, even after it had set,
When the pollen-dusted blossoms of the cherry tree
Trembled, silently, as I wrote each line.
And old Ez, so silent in those days,
Where are the lips his lay upon when he smooched
The brazen ideogram of Fenollosa, & had
To chew him up, gnawed bones in a sack

Buried under a plum tree, the sun sagging behind
Mt. Taishan? This is not China, but America—
Where the past, when you first learn to take it
As your own, throws all the cultures in the world
Into the big flat trunk of your SUV
As you ride past, & wave your flag. Gary's driving.
Even the Christmas lights are made in China.
People are shopping for images. Each hand,
With its pink eager fingers, with a twenty
Clutched inside it, reaching up
To stroke a bolt of silk, or shut a mouth,
Just the same as every other hand.
You know how silence turns a poem Chinese,
Leaving all the best bits showing through:
Suzie Wong, old Ezra, egg foo yung;
A cheongsam holding my body still?
Inside, it's quiet, dainty, & the Year of the Dog.
My ideograms are turning white.
I always thought they'd stay like that.
I always thought they wouldn't dare to speak.

Chinese Silence No. 87

after Ezra Pound, "Epitaphs"

E.F.

E.F. loved the Chinese and their silence.
Alas, he died Japanese.

E.P.

And E.P. also died silent.
He tried to embrace an empire
In an ideogram.

Chinese Silence No. 88

after Ezra Pound, "Liu Ch'e"

This brand of silk has been discontinued.
Anthologies litter the court-yard.
There is no sound of English, and its words
Sag into each other like swill,
And he the interpreter of silence lies beneath them:

A thief with the mask of Confucius.

Chinese Silence No. 89

after Ezra Pound, "Fan-Piece, for Her Imperial Lord"

O fan of white folk,
        clean as blood on the axe-blade,
You hide behind Chinese eyes.

Chinese Silence No. 90

after Ezra Pound, "Ts'ai Chi'h"

The Chinese fall in the kettle,
    the yellow-colored bone-strings,
Their silence clings to the spoon.

Chinese Silence No. 91

after Ezra Pound, "The Beautiful Toilet"

Poo, poo say the poems of our fathers
And their words have overfilled our dank outhouse.
And within, the poet, in the purging of his gut,
Green, green of face, defecates, locking the door.
Queasy, he puts forth a queasy hand;

And he was American in the old days,
And he has become a Chinese,
Who now squats silently down
Above a blooming throne.

Chinese Silence No. 92

after Ezra Pound, "Exile's Letter"

To Tom S. of Missouri, possum friend, clerk at Lloyd's.
Now I remember that you rang a silent bell
By the foot of the bridge at the River "Thames."
With dull roots and dried tubers, you wrote poems and laments
And grew more English month on month, bowing to kings and princes.
Americans came drifting in from the sea and from the west border,
And with them, and with me especially
Everything was pig-headed,
And I made hay from poppy-cock and painted adjectives,
Just so we could start a new fellowship,
And we all escaped our personalities, without expressing them.
And then I was sent off to Rapallo,
            trailed by children,
And you to your desk at Faber-Faber,
Till we had nothing but China and silence in common.
And then, when modernism had come to its worst,
We wrote, and published in Po-Etry,
Through all the one hundred kinds of shy and whispering silence,
Into a poem of a thousand blank pages,
That was the first heave;
And into ten thousand poems full of Chinese reticence.
And with chafing saddle and the bit in his mouth
Out from the East came Confucius and his philosophy,
And there came also the "True-man" Ben-it-o to awe me,
Playing in the death-mask of Jefferson.
In the botched houses of Europe they gave us more foetid music,
Clanging instruments, like the sound of a myriad dying.
My forefather Confucius got me drunk and I danced
            because my savage mind wouldn't keep still
Without his music playing,
And I, wrapped in silence, woke up with my head on his lap,
And my voice returning to me from every radio,
And before the end of the broadcast we scattered like cards, or bombs,
I had to be off to China, so far across my desktop,
You back to your London-bridge.

And our Roosevelt, who was brave as a rodent,
Was president in Washing Town, and let in the usurious rabble.
And one May he sent the soldiers for me,
            despite the long distance.
And what with broken idols and so on, I won't say it wasn't hard going,
Over roads twisted like my brain's folds.
And I was still going, late in the war,
            with defeat blowing in from the North,
Not guessing how little I knew of the cost,
            and how soon I would be paying it.
And what a reception:
Steel cages, two books set on a packing-crate table,
And I was caught, and had no hope of escaping.
And you would walk out with me to the northeast corner of my cell,
Toward the Alpine peak, with clouds about it as foul as London air,
With you whispering, *and with a bang, not a whimper,*
With glasses like dinner-plates, glowing grass-green in the darkness,
Pleasure-fasting, with women, coming and going without speech,
With the dandruff-flakes falling like snow,
And the hyacinth girls eating lunch in silence,
And the sea, knee-deep, reflecting white eyebrows—
Eyebrows turned white are an awful sight in the sunlight,
Hideously aged—
And the sea-girls singing back at us,
Drowning in seaweed brocade,
And the wind twisting the song, and desiccating it,
Covering our eyes with dust.
            And this is the way the world ends.
            With a bang, not with a whimper.
I went up to the court for prosecution,
Tried standing mute, offered a madman's song,
And got no conviction,
            and went back to Saint Elizabeth's
            Committed.
And once again, later, you stood at the foot of my bed,
And then the visit ended, you went back to Bloomsbury,
And if you ask if I recall that parting:

It is like the hair falling from my hieratic head,
            Confused...Whirl! Centripetal! Mate!
What is the use of talking, until I end my song,
I end my song in the dark.
I call in the nurse,
Hold the pill in my hand
            As she says, "Take this,"
And swallow it down, silent.

Chinese Silence No. 93

after Ezra Pound, "The City of Choan"

The Chinese are aloof in their silence.
The Chinese are gone, my poem flows on alone.
Brushstrokes and images
Paper over the rutted road
        where lay the fallen house of Poe.
The silk gowns and small shoes of Cathay
Are now the base of my dung-heap.

The Three Principles of Imagism fell through my fingers.
The spite of the White House
        split my mind in two.
Now high bars cover the windows
And I can not see China afar
And I am mad.

Chinese Silence No. 94

after Ezra Pound, "A Ballad of the Mulberry Road"

The sun has gone down on the "thing itself"
To look on the short men of China,
For they have a daughter named Kuanon
        (pretty girl)
Whose name I have just made up: "Silent One,"
For she feeds poems to maggots.
She gets them from the rough hem of my gown.
With gut strings she breaks the warp of my poems,
She makes the claptrap of my poems
        with the boughs of Frazer,
And she piles skulls up on the back side of my fan-piece.

Her earrings are made of ears.
Her underskirt is a black steamship hull.
Her overskirt is a notebook dyed poppy-red.
And when Americans hear her silence
        They throw down their poems,
They rend and curse their manuscripts.

Chinese Silence No. 95

after Ezra Pound, "In a Station of the Metro"

The apparition of these Chinese in a crowd:
Peril in a white, silk shroud.

Chinese Silence No. 96

after Ezra Pound, "Lament of the Frontier Guard"

By the Golden Gate, the fog swirls full of self,
Hungry from the beginning of America until now!
Forests fall, the sky grows yellow with pollution.
We built towers and towers
            to exploit the profitable land:
Derelict factories, TV, the wide waistlines.
There is no there left to this here.
Faces white as a thousand snows,
High hipsters, bored from brow to ass;
What can end our ennui?
What can soothe our flaming imperial anger?
What can make us a nation of bums and dharma-bums?
Chinese things.
A garish shame, turned to jade-ravenous consumption,
A riot of po-men swarm over the middle kingdom,
Three hundred and thirteen million,
And silence, silence like pain.
Silence to take, and silence, silence performing,
Deafening, deafening poems,
And no children of China within them,
            No longer caring if we cause offense.
Ah, now shall you all hear the dreary silence at the Golden Gate,
With Confucius's name forgotten,
And our mothers turned into tigers.

Chinese Silence No. 97

after Ezra Pound, "Song of the Bowmen of Shu"

Here we are, mimicking the old Chinese
And saying: Do we have to go back to our country?
Here we are because we have old E.P. for our Whitman,
We have no compunction exploiting these mongrels.
We ape the soft Chinese,
When anyone says "Li Po," the others are full of silence.
Silent guys, silence is strong, we are manly and wistful.
Our fame is not yet secure, no one knows who Billy Collins is.
We all become Chinese.
We say: Will we be made to go back to America?
There is no joy in our Western airs, we have no compunction.
Our silence is sweeter, so we would not return to our country.
What fragrance has come from our bottom?
Whose arrogance? The Ezra's.
Poems, his poems even, are tired. They were wrong.
We have nothing left, three anthologies a month.
Goddam, his poems are tired.
The Chinese are in them, the Americans swear by them.
The readers are well trained, the Chinese have ivory skin and minds
  composed of brushstrokes.
The enemy is literate, we must be middlebrow.
When we set out, the bookshelves were sagging with shame,
We come back with a show,
We go shyly, we are shifty and sneaky,
Our minds are full of silence, who will know we are thieves?

Chinese Silence No. 98

after Ezra Pound, "To-Em-Mei's 'The Unmoving Cloud'"

I

The tailpipe sputtered and sputtered,
            and the car stalls and stalls,
The eight cylinders of the engine
            are all melted into one morass,
And the potholed road peters out.
I stop in a room at the Motel East, quiet, quiet,
I rub my belly and whine.
My friends are deranged, or in prison,
I bow my head and feel ill.

II

Car, car, and the tailpipe sputtered,
The eight cylinders of the engine are morass,
The potholed land looks like my liver.
            "Whine, whine, hear me whine!"
I drink in Eastern silence.
I think of talking to no man,
And no goat, no marriage, reproaches.

III

The Chinese in my east-copied garden
            are busting out with new poems.
They fill my bold new collection,
And they say my car and driver aren't moving
            because they can't run on bound feet.
The birds flutter to death in my teeth,
            and I think I have heard them singing,
"It is not that there is nothing to life
But we like this silence the best,
And whenever we try to speak
He says we are his to swallow."

Chinese Silence No. 99

after Ezra Pound, "The River-Merchant's Wife: A Letter"

When my verse was still laid out in straight pentameters
I played about with Provençal, growling ballads.
You whispered in cribbed notes, saying "horse,"
You drew about my feet the ideogram for "plum."
And we started writing in the style of Imagism:
Three small rules, without ornament or description.

In '15 I published My Li Po.
I tried to speak, and out came silence.
Lowering my head, I rammed the Great Wall.
Corrected a thousand times, I never looked back.

In '17 I said "Hang it all,"
I desired my poems to be garbed in yours
Forever and forever and forever.
Why should I be held to account?

In '45 I departed,
I went far into Wash-ing-ton, by the river of cold forgetting,
And you have not come to visit.
The critics make self-righteous noise at the door.

You bound my feet when you went out.
By my book now, the glosses grow, the different glosses,
Too many to clear them away.
The leaves fall and I try to keep them from falling.
The manuscript pages are turning yellow with peril
Under the covers of the West's sickbed;
They desert me. I grow silent.
If you are coming down through the narrows of the Potomac,
Please call me your Confucius,
And I will come out to meet you
As far as Arlington.

Chinese Silence No. 100

after Ezra Pound, Canto 49

For the hundred silences, and by you these verses:
Pain; empty notebooks; a collage,
Ire from silent crowds, dull pain in the sunlight
The cabin roof slants to one side.
Our needs are many; spent;
and our bamboo speech is still sleeping.

Awful moon; chills rise around fakes
a false sunset
Eating is like a delicate shroud,
a burr beneath footsoles; and through it
sharp filed teeth of the Chinaman,
a cold silence to our needs.
Behind Bill the temple bell
cracks in the wind.
Failure past here is fatal; may survive to recover
Notes fade in drivel; wholly;
Sun drains away from the center.

Where bookbag catches the child
Cracked chimneys fall in the lost fight

Cries then no cur in the liver
And our purse is filled with jade
Small verse grows like a lamprey,
The thudding heart clots and grows old. And in China
they are a people of quiet.
Wild eyes dart to the drudge-cart,
Crowds gather about the soul of the butcher
Bards wither; grease drips out with the phantom
Books flutter over the translator's lampreys,
A blight grows on the mouth's good line;
where the young boys broke stones for ships.
In nineteen fifteen came Ezra to these chill fakes.
A blight grows on the mouth's bad line.

Poet by creating China shd. thereby get into canon?
This is poetry; this is modernism.
This tunnel still leads to Billy
though the old man built it for shelter

S A Y   M E N   R A N   S A Y
E A T   M A N   M A N   S A Y
ABYSS UNLESS T   O D I E
G A G   F U K U G A G   C O Y

Sun up; work
sundown; to work
dig well and drink of the people
dig field; eat of their poems
Imperial power is, and for us complicit

The hundredth; the country of stillness.
And the power over Chinese.

Acknowledgments

The following poems have been previously published:

Chinese Silence Nos. 1-15: *15 Chinese Silences* (Tinfish Press)
Chinese Silence Nos. 1, 8, 14, 21, 23, 27, 28: *Mantis*
Chinese Silence No. 6: *Kartika Review*
Chinese Silence Nos. 16, 37: *Lantern Review*
Chinese Silence Nos. 17, 18, 19: *SHAMPOO*
Chinese Silence Nos. 22, 24, 40, 46, 80: *Cordite Poetry Review*
Chinese Silence No. 26: *asia!*
Chinese Silence No. 92: *Poetry*

www.ingramcontent.com/pod-product-compliance
Lightning Source LLC
Chambersburg PA
CBHW051428090426
42737CB00014B/2865

* 9 7 8 1 6 8 5 7 1 2 2 2 8 *